Who I Am: Reflections From Ephesians 1 and 2

SEAN SLAGLE

New Castle, Indiana

WHO I AM: REFLECTIONS FROM EPHESIANS 1 AND 2

Published by Northside Books & Media, an imprint of AGF Publishing LLC, New Castle, Indiana.

ISBN: 978-1-955709-13-2

WORKS BY SEAN SLAGLE

CHRISTIAN FICTION

The Sixth Commandment

A Light in the Darkness and Other Stories

CHRISTIAN NON-FICTION

It Is Well with My Soul and Other Writings

CHRISTIAN DRAMA

The Carpenter's Daughter

The Christmas Word

A Primetime Christmas

Poems of the Passion

A Caroling We Will Go

Pontius Pilate

At the Cross

The Heavenly Host

The Summoning of Me

A Socialite Christmas

Son of God

Do You Believe in Miracles?

GENERAL YOUNG ADULT FICTION

Christmas Casualties (A Dirge for the Malice #3)

Fall Fatalities (A Dirge for the Malice #2)

Halloween Havoc (A Dirge for the Malice #1)

The Vale of Eden

A Dirge for the Malice

SCHOOL DRAMA

#GreatestLifeEver

Sleepy Hollow High School

POETRY

The Pen of a Skillful Writer and Other Poems

DEDICATION

To the men who were the inaugural participants of The Twelve.

Thank you for your Godly influence and allowing God to lead your lives.

CONTENTS

UNLOCKING YOUR IDENTITY IN CHRIST: USING THE BOOK AS A PERSONAL JOURNAL AND MEANS OF DISCOVERY

The journey of understanding your identity in Christ is transformative and empowering. As believers, we are called to delve deeper into our relationship with God, seeking to comprehend the vastness of His love and the richness of our identity in Him. A personal journal can be a powerful tool in this exploration, enabling you to record your reflections, revelations, and encounters with God's Word. It is my prayer that you will use this book as a personal journal and a means of discovery to uncover the beautiful truths of who we are in Christ and that you will be inspired to reflect on your relationship with God and help you explore the depths of your identity in Him.

As you read through the book, embrace the journaling process as an integral part of your spiritual growth. Allow your journal to become a safe space where you can be authentic, vulnerable, and open with God. Write freely and without judgment, pouring out your thoughts, emotions, and questions onto the pages.

To answer the given reflective questions, approach them with an open heart and a desire to grow in your understanding of your identity in Christ. Take time to reflect on the insights gained from the reading, pondering how they align with God's Word and resonate with your personal experiences.

As you record personal insights in the book or in your journal, be honest and vulnerable with God, acknowledging both areas of growth and areas that need further understanding. Consider practical ways to apply the revealed truths to your life, seeking to live out your identity in Christ more intentionally.

As you encounter new revelations and personal insights from the book, jot them down in your journal. These moments of clarity and understanding are essential in recognizing how God is speaking to your heart and unveiling His truth about your identity in Christ.

Consider how you can apply practical applications to your life, relationships, and daily choices. Use your journal as a place to brainstorm ways to integrate these truths into your daily walk with Christ.

The group discussion questions at the end of the book can be used in a group setting or as more personal questions. Engaging with group discussion questions in a group setting provides an opportunity to gain new perspectives and learn from others' insights. And you can bless others in the group by sharing your insights. If answering the questions as personal reflections, take time to ponder them in your journal. Engaging with these questions in either setting will deepen your understanding and provide a space for further reflection.

Whether you embark on this journey alone or as part of a small group study, journaling provides a valuable space for self-reflection, personal growth, and spiritual discovery. Embrace the process with a willing heart and an open mind, and watch as God unveils the beautiful truths of who you are in Christ.

Using this book as a personal journal and means of discovery is a transformative practice that allows us to uncover the depths of your identity in Christ. As you journal, open yourself up to the Holy Spirit's guidance, allowing Him to reveal His truths and love to you in new and profound ways. The process of journaling enables you to internalize these truths and integrate them into your life, resulting in a more intimate relationship with God and a deeper understanding of your identity and who you are.

PRE-STUDY/REFLECTIVE QUESTIONS

1. Why do you think people struggle with issues of identity?

____

____

____

____

____

2. How do you see yourself?

____

____

____

____

____

____

3. Why do people tend to be so hard on themselves when it comes to who they are as a person?

____

____

____

____

____

____

4. Write a prayer asking God to speak to your heart as you go through these reflections and meditations. Ask Him to work in your life and to help you see yourself as He sees you. Be sure to thank Him for this opportunity and for all that He has done for you.

5. What do you hope to gain from reading these reflections and meditating on the scriptures?

1

I am blessed!

"Praise be to the God and Father of our Lord Jesus Christ, who has blessed us in the heavenly realms with every spiritual blessing in Christ" (Ephesians 1:3). Saying I'm blessed isn't enough. I am blessed with every spiritual blessing in Christ. He doesn't withhold any from me. He uses EVERY SPIRITUAL BLESSING when it comes to me. When the devil comes at me with all of my faults and failures, when I don't think I'm good enough, when I don't think I have what it takes to accomplish the task before me, I must remember that I am blessed beyond measure. Not only blessed with a few spiritual blessings from Christ but from EVERY SPIRITUAL BLESSING.

But what does that mean – EVERY SPIRITUAL BLESSING? Paul goes on to discuss the spiritual blessings through the opening chapters of Ephesians. It is these blessings that I look at and am encouraged. God holds nothing back from me. Everything has been granted to me as an inheritor of His kingdom. He blesses me with everything within His power – the power of the Creator of the universe who spoke all things into existence, who defeated death, who brought me into a close, personal relationship with Him.

The all-powerful God cares and loves me no matter my faults and failures. He is there to pour EVERY SPIRITUAL BLESSING upon me for His glory and good will. That is one part of who I am – I am blessed by the God of all creation who blesses me with EVERY SPIRITUAL BLESSING in Christ. All praise to Him!

I AM BLESSED!

1. From your favorite Bible translation, write down Ephesians 1:3.

____

____

____

____

____

2. What truths do you learn from this verse?

____

____

____

____

____

____

3. How does the fact that God blesses you help you as you go about your daily activities?

____

____

____

____

____

____

4. What other thoughts or ideas come to mind as you meditate over this truth from Ephesians 1:3?

5. Take a moment to write a prayer. Be sure to thank God for blessing you.

6. Other notes:

2

I am chosen!

Let me say that again – I am chosen!

"For he chose us in him before the beginning of the world" (Ephesians 1:4). In a world of rejection – from jobs, promotions, relationships, I can stand firm that the only One who matters chose me. He paved the way for me to have a relationship with Him – a deep, personal relationship brought about through a daily walk with the creator of the universe, all because He chose me. He sought me out. He sent His Son to die on the cross for all the stupid, prideful stuff I do and think, all so I could come into a relationship with Him.

He sent his spirit to dwell in my heart so that I could remain in fellowship with Him. All because He chose me. I was important to Him. I mean something. I am worthy. All because He chose me. He chose me. I'm not worthy. I don't do anything to earn such a great honor. All I did was accept Jesus as my personal Lord and Savior. I felt an emptiness in my soul that longed to be filled. And I was only able to fill that emptiness because He chose me.

God chose to come into a relationship with me, just as He does with all people. He wants "all people to be saved and come to a knowledge of the truth" (1 Timothy 2:4, NIV). He chose to make a way for all people to come into a relationship with Him. All that is required of us is to put aside our pride and repent of our sins and accept Jesus as our Savior. God is patient with us, giving us time and opportunity to make this decision, because He doesn't want "anyone to perish, but everyone to come to repentance" (2 Peter 3:9, NIV).

God chose me. God chose you. God chose the members of your family, your neighbors, your co-workers. He chose us over all things, but the choice lies with us in whether or not we choose Him as our personal Lord and Savior. 1 Peter 2:9-10 explains that we are chosen by God – "But you are a chosen people, a royal priesthood, a holy nation, God's special possession, that you may declare the praises of him who called you out of darkness into his wonderful light. Once you were not a people, but now you are the people of God; once you had not received mercy, but now you have received mercy."

That mercy is a free gift from God. Something He prepared for all people – a way to come into fellowship with Him. All because He chose us.

What is that way to fellowship? Jesus said, "I am the way and the truth and the life. No one comes to the Father except through me" (John 14:6). God prepared that way though His Son. There had to be a sacrifice for sin. The Hebrews sacrificed unblemished animals as a payment for their sins. Then Jesus came and lived a perfect life, never sinning, never having a blemish. He became the sacrifice once and for all for everyone. God chose us when He sent His Son to shed His blood for our sins. "He is the atoning sacrifice for our sins, and not only for ours but also for the sins of the world" (1 John 2:2).

Even if a person doesn't choose to accept the gift of salvation, God still chose them; Jesus still died for them. But He allows us the free will to choose. As for me, I am thankful that I accepted his free gift of salvation. And I can feel blessed that He chose me, that He loved me enough to make a way for me to have fellowship with Him. He chose me!

GOD DOES NOT CHOOSE US FOR WHO WE ARE, OR HOW QUALIFIED WE ARE, BUT RATHER FOR WHO HE IS AND WHAT HE IS PERMITTED TO DO THROUGH OUR LIVES

A.W. Tozer, author and preacher

GOD DID NOT CHOOSE US BECAUSE WE WERE WORTHY, BUT BY CHOOSING US HE MAKES US WORTHY.

Thomas J. Watson, businessman

THE SOVEREIGN ELECTING GRACE OF GOD CHOOSES US TO REPENTANCE, TO FAITH, AND AFTERWARDS TO HOLINESS OF LIVING, TO CHRISTIAN SERVICE, TO ZEAL, AND TO DEVOTION.

Charles H. Spurgeon, preacher

I AM CHOSEN!

1. From your favorite Bible translation, write down Ephesians 1:4.

____

____

____

____

____

2. What truths do you learn from this verse?

____

____

____

____

____

____

3. How does the fact that God chose you help you as you go about your daily activities?

____

____

____

____

____

____

4. What other thoughts or ideas come to mind as you meditate over this truth from Ephesians 1:4?

5. Take a moment to write a prayer. Be sure to thank God for choosing you.

6. Other notes:

3

I am holy and blameless in His sight!

How in the world is that true? I am far from holy and there is much blame that can be heaped on my shoulders. Yet God chose me in Christ to be holy and blameless in His sight. That just blows my mind. There's no way. But I have to believe the truth of God's word. "For he chose us in him before the creation of the world to be holy and blameless in his sight" (Ephesians 1:4).

We are holy and blameless because we are in Him – in Christ. This has nothing to do with our abilities or spirituality but everything to do with Christ's perfection as the holy and blameless sacrifice to die for our sins. As Christians, we are clothed in Christ. His holiness and blamelessness are bestowed upon us through God's grace.

What an act of love! I am blessed because God chose me to be in a relationship with Him. And when He looks at me, He doesn't see the wretched sinner but a new creation in Christ – one that is holy and blameless – not because of anything I have done but because of what Jesus did for me, because of what grace allowed to be applied to me.

God's grace and Christ's holiness and blamelessness are not for my abuse or right to live in sin. It is because of God's grace that I have accepted Christ as my Savior – and in doing so, present my body "as a living sacrifice, holy and pleasing to God" (Romans 12:1). It's because of His love for me that I can live a life of love toward God and my fellow humans. And when I mess up, I can rest in knowing that God sees me as holy and blameless in Christ.

I AM HOLY AND BLAMELESS!

1. From your favorite Bible translation, write down Ephesians 1:4.

2. What truths do you learn from this verse?

3. How does the fact that God sees you as holy and blameless help you as you go about your daily activities?

4. What other thoughts or ideas come to mind as you meditate over this truth from Ephesians 1:4?

____

____

____

____

____

5. Take a moment to write a prayer. Be sure to thank God for making you holy and blameless in His sight.

____

____

____

____

____

____

____

____

6. Other notes:

____

____

____

____

____

4

I am an adopted child of God!

"In love he predestined us for adoption to sonship through Jesus Christ, in accordance with his pleasure and will" (Ephesians 1:4-5). He chose me to be part of His family. To quote a footnote – "The Greek word for *adoption to sonship* is a legal term referring to the full legal standing of an adopted male heir in Roman culture." I have all the rights and privileges as a child of God.

The great act of love, as making us heirs, began before the creation of the world. And the inheritance which has been bestowed upon us is "every spiritual blessing" (1:3). These blessings are recounted throughout these first chapters in Ephesians, and especially in chapter 1, which seems to be Paul's purpose in writing this section.

As you read through this book, we will look at each of these blessings and what those blessings say about us. Here is an overview of the blessings listed in chapter 1:

Blessed (3)	Chosen (4)	Holy and Blameless (4)
Loved (4)	Adopted (5)	Given Grace (6)
Redeemed (7)	Forgiven (7)	Lavished on (7-8)
Knowledgeable (9)	Predestined (11)	Marked with a Seal (13)
Hopeful (18)	Valued (18)	Powerful (19-20)

And that's just the first chapter. When we see ourselves as God sees us, we begin to live the blessed life that He meant for us to live.

I AM AN ADOPTED CHILD OF GOD!

1. From your favorite Bible translation, write down Ephesians 1:4-5.

____

____

____

____

____

2. What truths do you learn from these verses?

____

____

____

____

____

____

3. How does the fact that God adopted you as His child help you as you go about your daily activities?

____

____

____

____

____

____

4. What other thoughts or ideas come to mind as you meditate over this truth from Ephesians 1:4-5?

____

____

____

____

____

5. Take a moment to write a prayer. Be sure to thank God for adopting you into His family.

____

____

____

____

____

____

____

____

6. Other notes:

____

____

____

____

____

5

I am loved! (Ephesians 1:4)

The Bible is truly a love story between God and His people. When sin came into the world, His justice demanded a punishment for sin, so He provided a way for man to have fellowship with Him. He gave man the law so they would know what sin was and what was hindering them in their relationship. God even provided the acts of sacrifice as a penance for sin.

But He always had a bigger, deeper plan. Because God loved me so much, he sent His only Son that if I believe in Him, I won't perish but have eternal life (John 3:16). The system He set up paved the way for the coming of Christ and His ultimate sacrifice. His love provided a way for me to be in relationship with Him.

At its core, sin changed man's relationship with God – that's why Adam and Eve first hid from God, that is why they had to be removed from the Garden of Eden and forced to work the land and feel the pains of childbirth. And sin also brought death. "For the wages of sin is death, but the gift of God is eternal life through Jesus Christ our Lord" (Romans 6:23).

That's how much God loves us. That's how much God wants to be in relationship with us. While His goodness and righteousness demand justice, He not only provided a way to rectify the sins but paid the ultimate price once and for all. God loves me so much that He gave the gift of "eternal life through Jesus Christ our Lord" (Romans 6:23). "God demonstrated his own love toward us, in that while we were sinners, Christ died for us" (Romans 5:8).

And because of that love that He poured out for me, all I have to do is confess with my mouth that Jesus is Lord, and believe in my heart that God raised Him from the dead, and I will not only be saved from eternal punishment (Romans 10:9) but will come into a relationship with the God of the universe that loves me beyond measure, that adopts me as His son with full rights to inheritance, that sees me as holy and blessed because of the price His Son paid, for there is "no condemnation for those who are in Christ Jesus" (Romans 8:1).

Through this everlasting love, I will be in relationship with God for all of eternity. I can hold to this promise stated by the Apostle Paul: "For I am convinced that neither death nor life, neither angels nor demons, neither the present nor the future, nor any powers, neither height nor depth, nor anything else in all creation, will be able to separate (me) from the love of God that is in Christ Jesus our Lord" (Romans 8:38-39).

I am so very thankful that God loves me. That is part of who I am in Christ. I am loved by the Creator of the universe. Even with all my faults and same, He loves me.

He loves me!

GOD LOVES EACH OF US AS IF THERE WERE ONLY ONE OF US.

St. Augustine

THE LOVE OF GOD IS NOT CREATED – IT IS HIS NATURE.

Oswald Chambers, Scottish Evangelist

GOD IS UNCHANGING IN HIS LOVE. HE LOVES YOU. HE HAS A PLAN FOR YOUR LIFE. DON'T LET THE NEWSPAPER HEADLINES FRIGHTEN YOU. GOD IS STILL SOVEREIGN; HE'S STILL ON THE THRONE.

Billy Graham, American Evangelist

I AM LOVED!

1. From your favorite Bible translation, write down Ephesians 1:4.

2. What truths do you learn from this verse?

3. How does the fact that God loves you help you as you go about your daily activities?

4. What other thoughts or ideas come to mind as you meditate over this truth from Ephesians 1:4?

____

____

____

____

____

5. Take a moment to write a prayer. Be sure to thank God for loving you.

____

____

____

____

____

____

____

____

6. Other notes:

____

____

____

____

____

6

I am given grace!

Grace is the free and unmerited favor of God, as manifested in my salvation. There is nothing I can do to earn God's grace. It is "freely given to us in the One he loves" (Ephesians 1:6).

If it weren't for grace, I would get exactly what I deserve – which is punishment beyond comprehension. And the ultimate punishment would be an eternity separate from God. But God, because of the grace He has given me, says that He won't give me what I deserve but will give me that which I don't deserve, all because of the work Jesus did on the cross.

As a teacher, I have deadlines for assignments. If an assignment is turned in after that deadline, then it automatically loses a percentage of points. But I sometimes waive that punishment and offer the students grace, accepting the late work as if it met the prescribed standard. I do this because I want them to understand the concept of grace – the giving of something that is undeserved.

It can be a human trait to try and take advantage of grace, and really at our hearts, if we're being honest, we probably all do this to some level, almost daily. "I'll do this, even though I shouldn't. It'll be okay." And perhaps it seems okay because no punishment is readily apparent – and wouldn't that actually be grace multiplied on grace? Aren't we often child-like in pushing our heavenly Father's standards to see just how much we can get away with? A smack on the hand might cause us to withdraw for a moment, but then we soon head right back toward that standard, seeing if we can get by with it this time. But God is patient with us, extending grace far beyond the points that we would extend it for ourselves.

Instead of parking His grace to the limits, I want to stand with a thankful heart at the blessings His grace provides, especially when it's multiplied. I want to praise Him for His goodness and righteousness for extending grace when I'm far from deserving. Without His grace, I couldn't stand in His presence; He wouldn't hear my prayers; I wouldn't spend eternity with Him in heaven; He would judge me to eternal damnation. Praise be to Jesus for paying the price for my sins. Praise be to God for applying that sacrifice to my account and wiping it clean and doing so for free out of His love for me!

I AM GIVEN GRACE!

1. From your favorite Bible translation, write down Ephesians 1:6.

____

____

____

____

____

2. What truths do you learn from this verse?

____

____

____

____

____

____

3. How does the fact that God gives you grace help you as you go about your daily activities?

____

____

____

____

____

____

4. What other thoughts or ideas come to mind as you meditate over this truth from Ephesians 1:6?

5. Take a moment to write a prayer. Be sure to thank God for giving you grace.

6. Other notes:

7

I am redeemed!

The blood he shed on the cross paid the price for sin though the riches of God's graces (Ephesians 1:7).

God can't be in the presence of sin. His glory and majesty won't allow it. So, when sin came into the world, something had to be done to help bring us back into the presence of God; after all, we were created for the purpose of having a relationship with Him. Hebrews 9:22 says, "Without the shedding of blood there is no forgiveness." So, for that reason, Jesus came to live a perfect life and die on the cross to pay the penalty for me.

Redeem has many meanings, such as our Christian theology of being saved or delivered from sin and its consequences. But there is so much more going on here. Dictionary.com gives these definitions:

1. having been paid, recovered, brought back, or exchanged for money or other goods;

2. having been discharged or fulfilled;
3. having made amends for or overcome some wrongdoing or fault.

All these definitions fit when I think about what God did for me through the sacrifice of His son, when I think about how I can come to the Father and ask for forgiveness for my wrongdoings, how He pulls me into a relationship with Him even though I am unworthy of such grace.

My sins have been paid.

My soul has been recovered through His redemptive plan.

I have been brought back into a relationship with Him.

God exchanged the blood of Christ for my sins (past, present, and future).

God's grace discharged me from my guilt.

The payment for sin has been fulfilled through Christ.

Jesus made amends for all humanity.

Through Jesus, I can overcome my sinful nature.

All my faults have been wiped clean.

To say I am redeemed is to say a lot. God's redemptive work through the shedding of His Son's blood paved a way for me to come to the Father and have an eternal relationship with Him.

I AM REDEEMED!

1. From your favorite Bible translation, write down Ephesians 1:7.

____

____

____

____

____

2. What truths do you learn from this verse?

____

____

____

____

____

____

3. How does the fact that God redeems you help you as you go about your daily activities?

____

____

____

____

____

____

4. What other thoughts or ideas come to mind as you meditate over this truth from Ephesians 1:7?

____

____

____

____

____

5. Take a moment to write a prayer. Be sure to thank God for redeeming you.

____

____

____

____

____

____

____

____

6. Other notes:

____

____

____

____

____

8

I am forgiven!

Through the redemptive work of Christ's blood, I have "forgiveness of sins, in accordance with the riches of God's grace" (Ephesians 1:7). My sins are many. Even when I fight the good fight, the flesh, that sinful nature within me, sometimes wins. But that loss doesn't defeat me, because that loss has been wiped off the record book by the blood of Christ.

Forgiveness is such a strong element in my life, and the fact is that I receive it, not because of something I've done, but because of God's grace toward me. And receiving that grace is so easy that I sometimes have a hard time accepting the truth of it. But it really is that simple.

First, I must recognize and admit that I am a sinner. I may tend to think that I'm not that bad, that other people are worse than me, that they are the sinners. But I only deceive myself. "Indeed, there is no one on earth who is righteous, no one who does what is right and never sins" (Ecclesiastes

7:20). Isaiah even writes a harsh simile to drive home this point – "All our righteous acts are like filthy rags" (Isaiah 64:6). In other words, nothing I do hits the mark of God's standard, especially when it comes to being sin free.

Sin is anything I do that is wrong. It can be something as simple as taking something small that doesn't belong to me to something as big as taking someone's life. The cost for sin is death, but thanks be to God that He gave us the gift of eternal life through Christ Jesus our Lord (Romans 3:23). And that gift was mine when I called upon the name of the Lord (Romans 10:13).

I am forgiven. 1 John 1:9 assures me that if I confess my sins, God is faithful and just and will forgive me of my sins. I am thankful for God's unconditional love that forgives me of my wrongdoings.

I AM FORGIVEN!

1. From your favorite Bible translation, write down Ephesians 1:7.

2. What truths do you learn from this verse?

3. How does the fact that God forgives you help you as you go about your daily activities?

4. What other thoughts or ideas come to mind as you meditate over this truth from Ephesians 1:7?

____

____

____

____

____

5. Take a moment to write a prayer. Be sure to thank God for forgiving you.

____

____

____

____

____

____

____

____

6. Other notes:

____

____

____

____

____

9

I am lavished on!

God bestows on me something rich, elaborate, and luxurious in generous and extravagant quantities. The God of the universe cares enough about me to give me the greatest gifts, greater than I could ever expect and far richer than anything I deserve.

What are those luxurious, extravagant gifts? "In Him we have redemption through his blood the forgiveness of sins, in accordance with the riches of God's grace that he lavished on us" (Ephesians 1:7-8). He lavished redemption, forgiveness, and grace on me.

1 John 3:1 emphasizes this point, when John writes, "See what great love the Father has lavished on us, that we should be called children of God! And that is what we are! The reason the world does not know us is that it did not know him." God lavishes on me because He loves me. That is why He redeemed me. That is why He forgives me. That is why His grace

is poured out on me. No matter what I do or not do, He lavishes His eternal gifts on me.

Because of this lavished love, I should also extend forgiveness and grace to others in my life. That is how I reflect His work in me. Paul later writes in Ephesians, “Be kind and compassionate to one another, forgiving each other, just as in Christ God forgave you” (4:32). That is many times easier said than done, but this outpouring of compassion and forgiveness for others should be a by-product of Christ’s continued work in my life.

I AM LAVISHED ON!

1. From your favorite Bible translation, write down Ephesians 1:7-8.

2. What truths do you learn from this verse?

3. How does the fact that God lavishes on you help you as you go about your daily activities?

4. What other thoughts or ideas come to mind as you meditate over this truth from Ephesians 1:7-8?

5. Take a moment to write a prayer. Be sure to thank God for lavishing on you.

6. Other notes:

10

I am knowledgeable!

God made known to me "the mystery of his will according to his good pleasure, which he purposed in Christ, to be put into effect when the times reach their fulfillment" (Ephesians 1:9-10).

What is the great thing that I am knowledgeable about? What is the mystery of His will? It's the plan of salvation through Jesus. The knowledge of this salvation led me into an eternal relationship with Him.

How did I come to understand this "mystery of His will"? I first realized that I was a sinner, and that I was accountable to God for those sins in my life. And if I didn't do something to atone for those sins, then I was going to spend eternity in Hell. The only atonement for those sins is through Jesus Christ dying on the cross and shedding His blood. And then I called upon the Lord, asking Him to come into my life as my personal Lord and Savior and to save me from those sins.

Romans 10:9-10 says:

> If you declare with your mouth, "Jesus is Lord," and believe in your heard that God raised him from the dead, then you will be saved. For it is with your heart that you believe and are justified, and it is with your mouth that you profess your faith and are saved.

And later Paul assures me that "everyone who calls on the Lord will be saved" (Romans 10:13).

It is the revelation of this knowledge that not only saved me from damnation but led me into a relationship with Him. That's why it's so important that I share the knowledge of this mystery with others, so they can also find salvation and relationship. I praise God that someone showed me the way, and I pray that I can do that for others.

I AM KNOWLEDGEABLE!

1. From your favorite Bible translation, write down Ephesians 1:9-10.

____

____

____

____

____

2. What truths do you learn from this verse?

____

____

____

____

____

____

3. How does the fact that God makes you knowledgeable help you as you go about your daily activities?

____

____

____

____

____

____

4. What other thoughts or ideas come to mind as you meditate over this truth from Ephesians 1:9-10?

____

____

____

____

____

5. Take a moment to write a prayer. Be sure to thank God for lavishing on you.

____

____

____

____

____

____

____

____

6. Other notes:

____

____

____

____

____

11

I am predestined!

"In him we were also chosen having been predestined according to the plan of him who works out everything in conformity with the purpose of his will (Ephesians 1:11). From the beginning of time, God had a plan for me to come into relationship with Him. All of God's work with the Hebrews through the generations leading up to the coming of Jesus, Jesus' work and his passing it onto His disciples, the work of the Holy Spirit in the New Testament and consequently through the generations leading up to me, happened so that I could come into an eternal relationship with Him.

God had a plan in place, one that was predestined by His omniscience. And what is that plan? "For those God foreknew he also predestined to be conformed to the image of his Son, that he might be the firstborn among many brothers and sisters. And those he predestined, he also called; those he called, he also justified; those he justified, he also glorified" (Romans 8:29-30). For those of us who accepted Jesus as our Savior, He plans for us to be conformed to the image of Christ, and in Him we are called, justified, and glorified.

My faith walk should lead me to be more and more like Christ, in my actions, thoughts, and prayers. When I accepted His call to salvation, I was justified by my faith in Him. In other words, His righteousness became my righteousness and justice was served in the eyes of God. And because of this righteousness, I am glorified in order to spend eternity with Him.

That was the plan all along – so spend eternity with Him. That was the purpose of His work throughout the Bible. That was the purpose for Christ dying for my sins and conquering death with his resurrection. That is the purpose for the ministry of the Holy Spirit. It's all about relationship – God bringing me into a relationship with Him for all of eternity.

I AM PREDESTINED!

1. From your favorite Bible translation, write down Ephesians 1:11.

____

____

____

____

____

2. What truths do you learn from this verse?

____

____

____

____

____

____

3. How does the fact that God predestined you help you as you go about your daily activities?

____

____

____

____

____

____

4. What other thoughts or ideas come to mind as you meditate over this truth from Ephesians 1:11?

____

____

____

____

____

5. Take a moment to write a prayer. Be sure to thank God for predestining you.

____

____

____

____

____

____

____

____

6. Other notes:

____

____

____

____

____

12

I am included in Christ!

"And you also were included in Christ when you heard the message of truth, the gospel of your salvation" (Ephesians 1:13a).

As a believer, I am clothed in Christ's righteousness, and all rights granted to Him as the son of God. Through this nature, God blesses me with the gifts of heaven. The key to this relationship is that I am in Christ, that I am at one with Him, that His spirit guards my spirit on a daily, even moment-by-moment, basis.

Paul drives this point home throughout the first verses of Ephesians. Look at the many times he states this point in the letter:

In Christ Jesus 1:1

In Christ 1:3, 1:12, 1:13

Through Jesus Christ 1:5

In Him (1:7), 1:17, 1:13

Under Christ 1:10

I can have confidence in knowing that I am in Christ, and God counts His righteousness toward me.

I AM INCLUDED IN CHRIST!

1. From your favorite Bible translation, write down Ephesians 1:13a.

____

____

____

____

____

2. What truths do you learn from this verse?

____

____

____

____

____

____

3. How does the fact that God includes you in Christ help you as you go about your daily activities?

____

____

____

____

____

____

4. What other thoughts or ideas come to mind as you meditate over this truth from Ephesians 1:13a?

____

____

____

____

____

5. Take a moment to write a prayer. Be sure to thank God for including you in Christ.

____

____

____

____

____

____

____

____

6. Other notes:

____

____

____

____

____

13

I am marked with a seal!

"When you believed, you were marked in him with a seal, the promised Holy Spirit" (Ephesians 1:13b). God marks me as His chosen, as redeemed, as being saved through the mark of His seal of approval, His seal of authentication, His seal that can't be broken. That seal is the Holy Spirit that dwells in me.

When I accepted Jesus as my personal Lord and Savior, God put His seal on me and gave me His Spirit in my heart as a guarantee (2 Corinthians 1:22). The Holy Spirit gives me strength and power to live a life pleasing to God. It is through the Spirit that I commune and deepen my relationship with God.

God loves me so much that He sealed me with His Spirit so that I could continually walk with Him and talk with Him and pour out my heart to

Him. It is through the Spirit that I have a relationship with Him until He calls me into His presence for all eternity. The Spirit "is a deposit guaranteeing (my) inheritance until the redemption of those who are God's possession – to the praise of his glory" (Ephesians 1:14).

I AM MARKED WITH A SEAL!

1. From your favorite Bible translation, write down Ephesians 1:13b.

2. What truths do you learn from this verse?

3. How does the fact that God marks you with a seal help you as you go about your daily activities?

4. What other thoughts or ideas come to mind as you meditate over this truth from Ephesians 1:13b?

____

____

____

____

____

5. Take a moment to write a prayer. Be sure to thank God for marking you with a seal.

____

____

____

____

____

____

____

____

6. Other notes:

____

____

____

____

____

14

I am called to hope!

"I pray that the eyes of your heart may be enlightened in order that you may know the hope to which he has called you" (Ephesians 1:18). When I think of hope, it is often expressed as faith with a dash of uncertainty. "I hope it doesn't rain Saturday," which says that I don't want it to rain but I'm not so sure that it won't. That is the wrong way of thinking when it comes to the hope I have in Christ.

Hope isn't wishful thinking – it's confidence in what God has promised and I expect those promises to come to fruition. I don't wish they'll happen; I know they'll be fulfilled. My hope for eternal life doesn't carry the thought of maybe it'll happen or maybe it won't; my hope has the confidence that a place has been prepared for me, just as Jesus said.

So, God doesn't call me to wishful thinking. He calls me to be confident in Him, to trust in His Word, to obey His commands, to know Him fully.

Those things don't come with a wish or uncertainty. They come from confidence in the Almighty God, who reigns over all. That is the hope He called me into.

I AM CALLED TO HOPE!

1. From your favorite Bible translation, write down Ephesians 1:18.

____

____

____

____

____

2. What truths do you learn from this verse?

____

____

____

____

____

____

3. How does the fact that God called you to hope help you as you go about your daily activities?

____

____

____

____

____

____

4. What other thoughts or ideas come to mind as you meditate over this truth from Ephesians 1:18?

____

____

____

____

____

5. Take a moment to write a prayer. Be sure to thank God for calling you to hope.

____

____

____

____

____

____

____

____

6. Other notes:

____

____

____

____

____

15

I am powerful!

All the power of Jesus is given to me through the Holy Spirit. Paul writes, "I pray that the eyes of your heart may be enlightened in order that you may know the hope to which he has called you, the riches of his glorious inheritance in his holy people, and his incomparably great power for us who believe" (Ephesians 1:18-19). His incomparably great power is for me!

Paul leaves no doubt about what the power is. He goes on to write, "That power is the same as the mighty strength he exerted when he raised Christ from the dead and seated him at his right hand in the heavenly realms, far above all rule and authority, power and dominion, and every name that is invoked, not only in the present age but also in the one to come" (1:19-21). That same power that conquered death, that rules over all authorities forever, is the power God has granted to me through Christ.

Too often I walk in defeat. I feel I'm not good enough for this or that, but the truth is that God has granted me His power to conquer the things in my life. I can quote 1 John 4:4 – "Greater is he that is in you, than he that is in the world" (KJV) – but do I really realize the power He granted me? How much more could I accomplish for His kingdom if I lived in this power? How much more hopeful and joyful would my life be if I lived in His power?

I AM POWERFUL!

1. From your favorite Bible translation, write down Ephesians 1:18-19.

____

____

____

____

____

2. What truths do you learn from this verse?

____

____

____

____

____

____

3. How does the fact that God empowers you help you as you go about your daily activities?

____

____

____

____

____

____

4. What other thoughts or ideas come to mind as you meditate over this truth from Ephesians 1:18-19?

____

____

____

____

____

5. Take a moment to write a prayer. Be sure to thank God for empowering you.

____

____

____

____

____

____

____

____

6. Other notes:

____

____

____

____

____

16

I am valued!

God valued me enough to send His son to die for my sins. He called me to live a life of hope. He adopted me into His family and blessed me with "the riches of his glorious inheritance" (Ephesians 1:18). Because of my hope, I partake in His rich, glorious inheritance.

My earthly treasure doesn't matter; God cares about our spiritual treasures, which He bestowed upon us as an inheritance. My value comes from these spiritual things – things I don't deserve, things I didn't work for, things that come only from His grace, because He values me as His child and grants upon me His inheritance. "Having been justified by his grace, we (become) heirs having the hope of eternal life" (Titus 3:7).

I can walk through my daily life with the knowledge that God values me. Jesus died as a "deposit guaranteeing (my) inheritance" (Ephesians 1:14). This inheritance is rich in mercy and grace and love and power. His righteousness shines on me. And all these great blessings of God are given to me as a child of God. No one or nothing can take that away from me.

I AM VALUED!

1. From your favorite Bible translation, write down Ephesians 1:18.

2. What truths do you learn from this verse?

3. How does the fact that God values you help you as you go about your daily activities?

4. What other thoughts or ideas come to mind as you meditate over this truth from Ephesians 1:18?

____

____

____

____

____

5. Take a moment to write a prayer. Be sure to thank God for valuing you.

____

____

____

____

____

____

____

____

6. Other notes:

____

____

____

____

____

17

I am alive!

God in his rich mercy made me alive with Christ (Ephesians 2:5). Even though I was dead in my sins, following my own desires and those instilled in me by the world, God's spirit was at work in me. He wanted me to see the error of my ways, the error of my thinking, so that I would repent of those sins and turn to Him. He had already prepared a way for me, but I had to first realize the errors of my ways.

When I was born into the world, I was born into a sinful nature. I didn't have to be taught the wrong things to do, for they were already a part of me, but I had to be shown the right things to do. Just like all humanity, I sinned and fell short of the glory of God. Just like all humanity, I was dead in my transgressions. Just like all humanity, I gratified the cravings of the flesh; I followed my desires and thoughts. Like all humanity, I deserved wrath. But God . . . (That is one of my favorite phrases in the Bible – but God). I was dead in my sin.

But God had an answer. "But because of his great love for us, God, who is rich in mercy, made us alive with Christ even when we were dead in transgressions – it is by grace (I) have been saved" (2:4-5). His love redeemed me though grace when I asked for forgiveness, making me holy and blameless in Christ, therefore making me alive as an adopted child of God, sealing me with His Spirit.

It is that Spirit dwelling in me that make me alive. The emptiness of the sinful life, the void in my heart that tried to be filled with the vices of the world, is now filled with God's Spirit, making me a new creation – making me alive with Christ in a way that surpasses all human understanding.

I AM ALIVE!

1. From your favorite Bible translation, write down Ephesians 2:5.

2. What truths do you learn from this verse?

3. How does the fact that God makes you alive help you as you go about your daily activities?

4. What other thoughts or ideas come to mind as you meditate over this truth from Ephesians 2:5?

5. Take a moment to write a prayer. Be sure to thank God for making you alive.

6. Other notes:

18

I am raised up!

When I became saved, God raised me up with Christ and seated me in the heavenly realms with Him (Ephesians 2:6). This speaks to my eternal position in Christ. Even though I was once lowly and dead to sin, because of God's grace and salvation, I am now seated with Him in heaven.

Even though I continue to grow spiritually and in my knowledge of Him, my spiritual position has been set at the right hand of the Father. That can only be done through Jesus, and as Christians we are in Christ. I don't always feel like I'm sitting at God's right hand. When my physical condition, still attached to a sinful nature, fails, I rest assured that my spiritual condition is fixed on Him in the heavenly places. This gives me strength when things aren't going as well as they should. I can't get caught up focused on the problems of the physical. My identity isn't found there. My identity is found in Christ, who is sitting at the right hand of the Father, who has accepted me as His adopted child and seated me with His son. It is there that my identity lies. It is there that I have power and strength.

Being raised up in Christ, being positioned at His right hand in Christ, having status and privilege in Christ, isn't about my feelings or circumstances, my words and deeds; it's about faith that everything I need is in Christ, and because of that, I have favor and status with God.

I AM RAISED UP!

1. From your favorite Bible translation, write down Ephesians 2:6.

2. What truths do you learn from this verse?

3. How does the fact that God raises you up help you as you go about your daily activities?

4. What other thoughts or ideas come to mind as you meditate over this truth from Ephesians 2:6?

____

____

____

____

____

5. Take a moment to write a prayer. Be sure to thank God for raising you up.

____

____

____

____

____

____

____

____

6. Other notes:

____

____

____

____

____

19

I am God's handiwork!

God created me for a purpose. "For we are God's handiwork, created in Christ Jesus to do good works, which God prepared in advance for us to do" (Ephesians 2:10). My talents, gifts, experiences, and relationship with the Lord make me different from everyone else in the world.

I am unique. Because God created my inmost being, knitting me together in my mother's womb, I am fearfully and wonderfully made (Psalm 139:13-14), He has prepared work for me to do that honors and glorifies Him. That is where my purpose lies.

God told Jeremiah, "Before I formed you in the womb I knew you, before you were born I set you apart; I appointed you as a prophet to the nations: (1:5). That same handiwork applies to me. He formed me; He set me apart; He appointed me to do good works. Too many times I let fear get in the way of fulfilling the works He has prepared for me. I let my failures and defeats of the past stand as disqualifications when the only qualification needed has been given to me by the Creator of the universe, by the One who set all things in motion, by the One who created me as His handiwork.

What my fellow man thinks or says about me should not get in the way of doing the good works God prepared for me in advance. It is with a stronger resolve that I accomplish what He has set before me. The only voice I should care about is His voice, and perhaps in doing that He will one day say, "Well done, good and faithful servant!" (Matthew 25:23). The rest of the voices are just white noise to distract me from fulfilling my purpose in Him.

I refuse to let the voice of others, and even of myself, keep me from the good works He planned for me. May I stay in close relationship with the God of all creation to fulfill all that He would have me to do. May I silence the doubt and rejections and negativity that stand in my way. May I fight the good fight. May I finish the race. May I keep the faith. And to God be the glory.

I AM GOD'S HANDIWORK!

1. From your favorite Bible translation, write down Ephesians 2:10.

2. What truths do you learn from this verse?

3. How does the fact that you are God's handiwork help you as you go about your daily activities?

4. What other thoughts or ideas come to mind as you meditate over this truth from Ephesians 2:10?

____

____

____

____

____

5. Take a moment to write a prayer. Be sure to thank God for making you His handiwork.

____

____

____

____

____

____

____

____

6. Other notes:

____

____

____

____

____

20

I am brought near!

There was a time when God's covenants and promises were with Israel, "but now in Christ Jesus you who were once far away have been brought near by the blood of Christ" (Ephesians 2:13). The Old Testament promises are now the promises given to those who believe in Him. God brought me near so that I could fully come into a relationship with Him.

There was a time when I was far away from God because of the sin in my life. There were many things standing between me and God. But when I accepted Jesus as my Savior, Jesus wiped away those barriers as God brought me near. And His work of grace continues to remove the barriers my sinful nature tries to put up. As James says, "Submit yourselves, then to God. Resist the devil, and he will flee from you. Come near to God and he will come near to you" (4:7-8).

I am thankful for a God that brings me near to Him so that we can have a relationship. His grace makes the way. "Blessed are those you choose and bring near to live in your courts! We are filled with the good things of your house, of your holy temple" (Psalms 65:4).

I AM BROUGHT NEAR!

1. From your favorite Bible translation, write down Ephesians 2:13.

2. What truths do you learn from this verse?

3. How does the fact that God brings you near help you as you go about your daily activities?

4. What other thoughts or ideas come to mind as you meditate over this truth from Ephesians 2:13?

____

____

____

____

____

5. Take a moment to write a prayer. Be sure to thank God for bringing you near.

____

____

____

____

____

____

____

____

6. Other notes:

____

____

____

____

____

21

I am a fellow citizen!

"Consequently, you are no longer foreigners and strangers, but fellow citizens with God's people" (Ephesians 2:19). When I read the Old Testament, I see God working in the lives of the Hebrews, making covenants, laws and promises with them. While His purpose always included me as a non-Hebrew (Gentile), when Christ came, died on the cross and rose from the grave, He brought all of humanity into one body.

Through Jesus, Hebrews and Gentiles alike have access to the Father by the Spirit, therefore bringing all of us together as God's people. So, when I look at God's work in the Old Testament, that work also applies to me and my faith – it is all part of the story that comes together in my salvation and relationship with Him.

Even the church started as a Hebrew movement, meeting and teaching in the synagogues, but just as Jesus commanded, the gospel went into all the world making disciples of all nations (Matthew 28:19). In doing so, the gospel made all Christians fellow citizens with God's people. The heritage that once belonged only to the Hebrews has now become my heritage, which in turn strengthens and challenges my faith in Him.

I AM A FELLOW CITIZEN!

1. From your favorite Bible translation, write down Ephesians 2:19.

____

____

____

____

____

2. What truths do you learn from this verse?

____

____

____

____

____

____

3. How does the fact that God makes you a fellow citizen help you as you go about your daily activities?

____

____

____

____

____

____

4. What other thoughts or ideas come to mind as you meditate over this truth from Ephesians 2:19?

5. Take a moment to write a prayer. Be sure to thank God for making you a fellow citizen.

6. Other notes:

22

I am a member of God's household!

"Consequently, you are no longer foreigners and strangers, but fellow citizens with God's people and also members of his household built on the foundation of the apostles and prophets with Christ Jesus himself as the chief cornerstone" (Ephesians 2:19-20).

When I was adopted into the family of God at the moment of my salvation, all of God's people became family. Family can sometimes be messy. Family can sometimes cause hurt and pain. Family also brings joy and companionship. Family brings a place of unconditional love – both from me and from others. Of course, sin messed up that which was intended to be perfect, but just because it isn't perfect doesn't make it any less important.

I am part of a family that includes my fellow church members, the other

Christians in my town, state, country, and world. The people at the church across town are family. The church in the next town is family. The church three states away is family. The church meeting secretly at someone's house in another country is family. We are all family – all waiting to be called up to that great reunion when Jesus returns.

From the moment of its inception after the ascension of Christ and the coming of the Holy Spirit, the church has been an all-inclusive community of believers from all backgrounds, starting with the Jews in Jerusalem, then those in Judea and Samaria, and then everyone to the ends of the earth. In the body of Christ there is no division of ethnicity or nationality; there is only one – those who have accepted Jesus as their personal Lord and Savior.

And as part of being in the family of God, my heritage comes from Jesus, the apostles, the prophets, the patriarchs, and all of the people who have continued to believe and share the gospel, building up the body of Christ. What started with Abraham and the other Hebrews led to Christ, then to the apostles, then to the church through the generations, and all the way down to me living here today – a gospel that not only saved me but made me a part of God's family.

I AM A MEMBER OF GOD'S HOUSEHOLD!

1. From your favorite Bible translation, write down Ephesians 2:19-20.

____

____

____

____

____

2. What truths do you learn from this verse?

____

____

____

____

____

____

3. How does the fact that God makes you a member of His household help you as you go about your daily activities?

____

____

____

____

____

____

4. What other thoughts or ideas come to mind as you meditate over this truth from Ephesians 2:19-20?

5. Take a moment to write a prayer. Be sure to thank God for making you a member of His household.

6. Other notes:

23

I am a dwelling!

"And in him you too are being built together to become a dwelling in which God lives by his spirit" (Ephesians 2:22). When I accepted Jesus as my Lord and Savior, the Holy Spirit came to live within me. The Holy Spirit is the New Testament covenant, the seal of salvation. 1 Corinthians 3:16 says, "Do you not know that you are a temple of God and that the Spirit of God dwells in you?" (NASB).

The Holy Spirit lives in me. He helps me and guides me. Even in the Old Testament, Ezekiel prophesied, "I will give you a new heart and put a new spirit in you; I will remove from your heart of stone and give you a heart of flesh. And I will put my Spirit in you and move you to follow my decrees and be careful to keep my laws" (36:26-27). Part of God's predestined plan was to have the indwelling of the Holy Spirit in my life. Because He lives within me, I can discern the things I should do and not do. Jesus told His disciples, "When he, the Spirit of truth, comes he will guide you into all the truth" (John 16:13).

Jesus goes on to say that the Spirit will not speak on His own but only what He hears from Jesus, whom the Spirit glorifies because the flesh is at one with Jesus and the Father (John 16:14-15). So, Jesus speaks into my life through the Spirit, which makes it all the more important that I listen to His Spirit. "Those who live in accordance with the Spirit have their minds set on what the Spirit desires" (Romans 8:5).

I can live the life I was meant to live because God's Spirit lives in me. He gives me life and peace. If I am truly a believer in Christ, then I live in the realm of the Spirit, who gives life cause of righteousness.

And the greatest part of all – "If the Spirit of him who raised Jesus from the dead is living in you, he who raised Christ from the dead will also give life to your mortal bodies because of his Spirit who lives in you" (Romans 8:11).

I have a new life because of God's Spirit living in me!

I AM A DWELLING!

1. From your favorite Bible translation, write down Ephesians 2:22.

2. What truths do you learn from this verse?

3. How does the fact that God makes you a dwelling help you as you go about your daily activities?

4. What other thoughts or ideas come to mind as you meditate over this truth from Ephesians 2:22?

___

___

___

___

___

5. Take a moment to write a prayer. Be sure to thank God for making you a dwelling.

___

___

___

___

___

___

___

___

6. Other notes:

___

___

___

___

___

LAST WORD

As Paul continued his discourse about the Holy Spirit with the Romans, he also ties together what has been discussed in this book about who I am in the eyes of God. The Holy Spirit ties everything together, making me who I am. The ministry of the Holy Spirit breathes life into me and helps me accept all that I am to Him.

Here are points Paul makes in Romans 8:14-17:

- "For those who are led by the spirit of God are the children of God" (14). Because I belong to God, I have His Spirit to guide me.

- "The Spirit you received does not make you slaves, so that you live in fear again; rather, the Spirit you received brought about your adoption to sonship" (15). There is no reason to have fear in my life because I have been adopted by God and His Spirit lives within me.

- "The Spirit himself testifies with our spirit that we are God's children" (16). There is no doubt about who I am and to whom I belong.

- "Now if we are children, then we are heirs – heirs of God and co-heirs with Christ" (17). Because of my adoption as a child of God, all rights of inheritance have been granted to me.

Because of the work of the Holy Spirit in my life, the gifts of God are manifested, and I can live in victory knowing that I am all of these things.

I am blessed!

I am chosen!

I am holy and blameless in His sight!

I am an adopted child of God!

I am loved!

I am given grace!

I am redeemed!

I am forgiven!

I am lavished on!

I am knowledgeable!

I am predestined!

I am included in Christ!

I am marked with a seal!

I am called to hope!

I am powerful!

I am valued!

I am alive!

I am raised up!

I am God's handiwork!

I am brought near!

I am a fellow citizen!

I am a member of God's household!

I am a dwelling!

POST REFLECTIVE QUESTIONS

1. How did you see yourself before reading these reflections?

____

____

____

____

____

2. What has changed about the way you see yourself since reading these reflections and meditating on the verses?

____

____

____

____

____

____

3. In what other ways has God been working in your life during your time of study and meditation?

____

____

____

____

____

____

4. What is your next step after going through these reflections and meditations? What do you hope to gain from this next step?

5. How can you help others see themselves as God sees them?

6. Other notes:

AFTERWORD

On April 24, 2023, I attended our monthly men's discipleship group at church. We are pairing up and taking turns teaching each month for 10 months. This particular night's lesson was led by Dr. John Davisson and Ken Durham, our family life pastor. Their lesson centered around how we see ourselves compared to how God sees us. One of the exercises was to silently read through the opening chapters of Ephesians and list what God says about us. I was amazed to see how much was there – and I even had to ask for five more minutes to keep working on my list.

After that evening, I wanted to look back at what God said about me in Ephesians and to have time to reflect on each aspect. Starting on April 25th, I began using my morning devotion time to reflect upon these passages. There were days that were missed and other days that were taken by other reflections, but on May 27th I wrote my last reflection and the last word, which was needed because I saw the connection of the Holy Spirit's ministry to making me who I am in God's eyes.

About halfway through reflection writings I realized that they could be put together in a book to encourage and strengthen other believers. Whatever the book becomes or is used for is only for purposes He knows, but my motivation is to help others. Too often we are beat down by how others see us, and perhaps even more strongly and damaging is how we see ourselves. When we see ourselves as God sees us, a whole new image is formed, an image that can only be created through Jesus and the work of the Holy Spirit.

I believe that I am all 23 characteristics listed. I also believe there is much more about who I am in Christ. A month ago, I might have listed some of these but not with the full conviction I now have. I hope that you can believe in who God created you to be. I pray that through your acceptance of Jesus as your Lord and Savior that you can stand firm that you are a new creation in Him and that no matter your failures and successes, your identity is secure in Him.

With love,
Sean Slagle
May 28, 2023

GROUP DISCUSSION QUESTIONS

I AM BLESSED!

1. What does it mean to be blessed with every spiritual blessing in Christ?

2. How does the concept of being blessed beyond measure impact one's perspective on personal faults and failures?

3. In what ways can the assurance of receiving every spiritual blessing empower an individual in facing challenging tasks or situations?

4. What is the significance of God's willingness to grant every spiritual blessing and not withholding anything from His followers?

5. How does the belief in being blessed with every spiritual blessing affect one's understanding of their identity and relationship with God?

6. How can the knowledge of being blessed by the all-powerful God impact one's sense of worth and self-esteem?

7. In what specific ways do the spiritual blessings discussed in the book of Ephesians encourage and uplift the individual?

8. How does the idea of being blessed by the God of all creation with every spiritual blessing inspire gratitude and praise?

9. What role does the concept of being blessed with every spiritual blessing play in one's overall perspective on life and purpose?

10. How does the understanding of being blessed beyond measure influence one's approach to sharing God's love and blessings with others?

I AM CHOSEN!

1. What does it mean to be chosen by God and how does that impact your sense of worth and purpose?

2. How does the knowledge of being chosen by God counteract feelings of rejection or inadequacy in a world that often values achievement and external validation?

3. In what ways does the concept of being chosen by God influence your understanding of personal responsibility and accountability?

4. How does the idea of God choosing you and sending His Son as a sacrifice for your sins affect your perception of His love and grace?

5. Reflect on the significance of God's patience and desire for all people to come to repentance. How does that impact your view of evangelism and sharing the message of salvation?

6. How does the concept of being chosen by God for a purpose impact your understanding of your own identity and role in His kingdom?

7. In what ways does the assurance of being chosen by God inspire gratitude and a desire to live a life that honors Him?

8. How does the understanding of God's choice and sacrifice through Jesus Christ deepen your appreciation for the gift of salvation?

9. Reflect on the balance between God's choice and human free will. How does this tension shape your understanding of faith and personal decision-making?

10. How can the knowledge of being chosen by God influence your relationships with others, your attitudes towards forgiveness, and your willingness to extend mercy?

I AM HOLY AND BLAMELESS IN HIS SIGHT!

1. How does the concept of being holy and blameless in God's sight challenge your perception of your own flaws and shortcomings?

2. Reflect on the idea that your holiness and blamelessness are not based on your own abilities or achievements, but on Christ's sacrifice and God's grace. How does this perspective shift your understanding of your identity?

3. In what ways does the belief in being holy and blameless in God's sight impact your behavior and choices in daily life?

4. How does the assurance of being seen as holy and blameless by God inspire gratitude and motivate you to live a life of love and righteousness?

5. Reflect on the tension between recognizing your imperfections and simultaneously embracing your identity as holy and blameless in Christ. How does this tension influence your approach to personal growth and spiritual maturity?

6. How does the understanding of God's love and grace shape your response to your own failures and mistakes? How does it influence your attitude towards forgiveness and self-compassion?

7. In what ways can the belief in being holy and blameless impact your relationships with others and your ability to extend grace and forgiveness to those around you?

8. Reflect on the responsibility that comes with being seen as holy and blameless in God's sight. How does this understanding impact your commitment to living a life that reflects the character of Christ?

9. How can the belief in being holy and blameless in Christ transform your perspective on your own worth and value as an individual?

10. How does the truth of being holy and blameless in God's sight inspire awe and gratitude towards Him? How can you cultivate a deeper appreciation for His love and grace in your life?

I AM AN ADOPTED CHILD OF GOD!

1. Reflect on the concept of being adopted as a child of God. How does this understanding of your relationship with Him influence your sense of belonging and identity?

2. What does it mean to you to have all the rights and privileges as a child of God? How does this impact your perspective on your worth and value?

3. How does the truth of being predestined for adoption through Jesus Christ highlight God's love and intentionality in choosing you to be part of His family?

4. Reflect on the idea that the act of making you an heir and bestowing every spiritual blessing upon you began before the creation of the world. How does this perspective on God's eternal plan for your life shape your understanding of His purpose for you?

5. In what ways does the belief in being an adopted child of God influence your daily life and decision-making? How does it inform your relationships, priorities, and values?

6. How does the understanding of being an adopted child of God contribute to your sense of security and assurance in your faith journey?

7. Reflect on the significance of being part of God's family and the implications it has for your relationships with other believers. How does this understanding foster a sense of unity and community within the body of Christ?

8. How can the truth of being an adopted child of God inspire gratitude and praise in your life? In what ways can you express your appreciation for His love and grace?

9. How does the belief in being an adopted child of God impact your understanding of forgiveness and reconciliation? How does it shape your willingness to extend love and grace to others?

10. Reflect on the responsibility that comes with being an adopted child of God. How does this understanding influence your desire to live a life that honors Him and reflects His character?

I AM LOVED!

1. How does the understanding of God's love for you shape your perception of yourself and your worth?

2. Reflect on the depth of God's love demonstrated through the sacrifice of His Son, Jesus Christ. How does this profound act of love impact your relationship with Him?

3. In what ways does the truth of being loved by God inspire gratitude and awe in your life? How can you cultivate a greater appreciation for His love?

4. How does the belief in God's unconditional love for you influence your response to sin and the need for forgiveness? How does it affect your understanding of His grace and mercy?

5. Reflect on the statement that there is "no condemnation for those who are in Christ Jesus" (Romans 8:1). How does this truth empower you to live a life free from guilt and shame?

6. How does the knowledge of God's everlasting love for you provide comfort and assurance during times of difficulty, doubt, or fear?

7. In what ways can you actively receive and embrace God's love in your daily life? How can you deepen your personal experience of His love?

8. Reflect on the transformative power of God's love in your relationships with others. How does His love compel you to love and show compassion to those around you?

9. How does the belief in being loved by God impact your self-image and the way you treat yourself? How can you extend love, grace, and kindness to yourself as a reflection of His love?

10. Reflect on the promise that nothing can separate you from the love of God in Christ Jesus. How does this truth provide comfort and hope in challenging circumstances?

I AM GIVEN GRACE!

1. Reflect on your understanding of grace. How has this reflection deepened your appreciation for God's unmerited favor and the gift of salvation?

2. Consider the concept of receiving grace when you deserve punishment. How does this understanding of grace impact your relationship with God and your perception of His character?

3. Reflect on instances in your life where you have experienced and received grace from God. How did His grace transform your perspective, actions, or circumstances?

4. In what ways do you struggle with fully accepting and embracing God's grace? Are there areas in your life where you find it difficult to believe that His grace is sufficient?

5. How does the understanding of grace influence your relationships with others? How can you extend grace to those around you, mirroring the grace you have received from God?

6. Consider the balance between God's grace and personal responsibility. How does grace motivate you to live a life pleasing to God while understanding that it is not based on your own efforts or merits?

7. Reflect on the concept of grace as an invitation to a deeper relationship with God. How does receiving His grace inspire you to draw near to Him, seek His presence, and grow in intimacy with Him?

8. How can you cultivate a heart of gratitude for God's grace in your daily life? How can you actively express thankfulness for His unmerited favor and the blessings it brings?

9. Reflect on the role of repentance and forgiveness in experiencing God's grace. How does a humble and contrite heart enable you to receive His grace more fully?

10. How can you share the message of God's grace with others? In what ways can you demonstrate His grace and point others to the source of true forgiveness and redemption?

I AM REDEEMED!

1. Reflect on the concept of redemption. How does understanding that you have been redeemed through Christ's sacrifice deepen your understanding of God's love and His plan for your salvation?

2. Consider the significance of Jesus' shed blood on the cross for the redemption of your sins. How does this truth impact your perception of your worthiness and your ability to approach God?

3. Reflect on the definitions of redemption provided in the reflection. In what ways have you personally experienced these different aspects of redemption in your own life and relationship with God?

4. How does the understanding of being redeemed affect your identity as a believer? How does it shape your perspective on your past, present, and future, knowing that you have been brought back into a relationship with God through Christ?

5. Reflect on the freedom and forgiveness that comes from being redeemed. How does this understanding of redemption empower you to live a transformed life and overcome sin and its consequences?

6. Consider the magnitude of God's grace and mercy in the process of redemption. How does this knowledge impact your gratitude and reverence towards Him?

7. Reflect on the depth of God's love demonstrated through the act of redemption. How does this love inspire you to respond and live a life that honors and glorifies Him?

8. In what ways does the understanding of redemption shape your view of others? How does it influence your ability to extend forgiveness, grace, and love to those around you?

9. Reflect on the ongoing nature of redemption. How does the knowledge that Christ's redemption covers your past, present, and future sins provide comfort and assurance in your journey of faith?

10. How can you share the message of redemption with others? In what ways can you testify to the transformative power of Christ's redemption in your own life and invite others to experience the same freedom and forgiveness?

I AM FORGIVEN!

1. Reflect on your understanding of forgiveness. How does the concept of receiving forgiveness through God's grace impact your view of your own sins and shortcomings?

2. Consider the role of humility in receiving forgiveness. How does acknowledging your own sinfulness and recognizing your need for forgiveness deepen your appreciation for God's grace?

3. Reflect on the significance of Christ's redemptive work in relation to forgiveness. How does the understanding that your sins are forgiven through His sacrifice on the cross shape your understanding of the magnitude of God's love and mercy?

4. How does the assurance of forgiveness impact your daily life? In what ways does it provide comfort, encouragement, and motivation to strive for righteousness?

5. Reflect on the difference between worldly forgiveness and God's forgiveness. How does God's forgiveness differ from human forgiveness, and what does it mean for you to experience true and complete forgiveness from God?

6. Consider the relationship between confession and forgiveness. How does the act of confessing your sins to God contribute to receiving His forgiveness? How does this practice foster humility, accountability, and spiritual growth?

7. Reflect on the weight and consequences of sin. How does the knowledge that the cost of sin is death magnify the significance of God's forgiveness? How does it inspire gratitude and a desire to live a life that honors Him?

8. How does the truth of God's forgiveness impact your self-perception and your ability to extend forgiveness to others? In what ways does it shape your view of your own worthiness and the worthiness of others?

9. Reflect on the transformational power of forgiveness. How does the experience of receiving God's forgiveness empower you to let go of guilt, shame, and the burden of past mistakes? How does it enable you to walk in freedom and pursue a life of purpose and righteousness?

10. How can you share the message of God's forgiveness with others? In what ways can you extend forgiveness to those who have wronged you and be a conduit of God's grace and mercy in their lives?

I AM LAVISHED ON!

1. Reflect on the concept of being lavished upon by God. How does it make you feel to know that God's love and blessings are abundant, extravagant, and beyond what you deserve?

2. Consider the significance of the gifts of redemption, forgiveness, and grace that God lavishes upon you. How do these gifts impact your relationship with God and your understanding of His character?

3. Reflect on the depth of God's love as the motivation behind His generosity. How does understanding that God loves you and desires to lavish His blessings upon you shape your perspective on your worthiness and value in His eyes?

4. Consider the responsibility that comes with receiving God's lavish love. How does being the recipient of His generosity and grace inspire you to extend forgiveness and grace to others in your life?

5. Reflect on your willingness to receive and accept God's lavish love. Are there any barriers or hindrances that prevent you from fully embracing and experiencing the abundance of His blessings? How can you open your heart and receive His love more fully?

6. Consider how you can reflect God's generosity in your own life. In what ways can you demonstrate kindness, compassion, forgiveness, and grace to others, mirroring the love that God has lavished upon you?

7. Reflect on the impact of God's lavish love on your identity as a child of God. How does being called a child of God and experiencing His abundant love and blessings shape your understanding of your true identity and purpose?

8. Consider the awe and gratitude that should arise from experiencing God's generosity. How can you cultivate a heart of thankfulness and express your gratitude to God for His overflowing blessings in your life?

9. Reflect on the difference between the world's understanding of abundance and God's lavishness. How does God's lavish love transcend worldly measures of success, wealth, and material possessions? How can you align your priorities and desires with His lavishness rather than the world's standards?

10. How can you share the message of God's lavish love with others? In what ways can you demonstrate His extravagant love and blessings to those around you, inviting them to experience the richness of His grace?

I AM KNOWLEDGEABLE!

1. Reflect on the knowledge you have about the mystery of God's will. How has this understanding of salvation through Jesus impacted your life and your relationship with God?

2. Consider the process through which you gained this knowledge. How did you come to realize your need for salvation and understand the significance of Jesus' sacrifice on the cross? Reflect on the steps you took to accept Jesus as your personal Lord and Savior.

3. Reflect on the significance of calling upon the Lord and professing your faith in Jesus. How does this act of declaration and belief lead to salvation and justification according to Romans 10:9-10?

4. Consider the assurance given by Paul in Romans 10:13 that "everyone who calls on the Lord will be saved." How does this promise deepen your understanding of God's willingness to save and His desire for a relationship with every individual?

5. Reflect on the responsibility and privilege of sharing the knowledge of God's mystery with others. How can you effectively communicate the message of salvation and lead others to a relationship with God?

6. Consider the impact that someone sharing the knowledge of salvation had on your own life. How can you express gratitude for those who played a role in leading you to the knowledge of God's will? How can you pay it forward by being a source of knowledge and guidance for others?

7. Reflect on the importance of ongoing learning and growth in your knowledge of God and His will. How can you continue to deepen your understanding of Scripture and the principles of the Christian faith?

8. Consider the potential obstacles or doubts that may arise in your journey of knowledge and faith. How can you address these challenges and seek answers to your questions, strengthening your knowledge and trust in God?

9. Reflect on the transformative power of knowledge and how it shapes your worldview, values, and decisions. In what ways has your knowledge of God's will influenced your choices and actions?

10. How can you actively apply the knowledge you have gained about God's will in your daily life? How can you live out the principles and truths you have learned and allow them to guide your thoughts, words, and deeds?

I AM PREDESTINED!

1. Reflect on the concept of predestination and God's plan for your life. How does this understanding impact your perspective on your purpose and significance in the grand scheme of God's plan?

2. Consider the idea of being conformed to the image of Christ. In what ways has your faith walk led you to become more like Christ in your actions, thoughts, and prayers? Reflect on areas where you have seen growth and areas where you still strive to align with Christ's character.

3. Reflect on your acceptance of Jesus' call to salvation and how it has justified you in the eyes of God. How does the righteousness of Christ become your righteousness through faith? How does this understanding of justification impact your relationship with God?

4. Consider the promise of being glorified in Christ and spending eternity with Him. How does this perspective shape your perspective on the challenges and trials you face in life? How does the hope of eternity impact your daily choices and priorities?

5. Reflect on the overarching purpose of God's work throughout the Bible, from the Old Testament to the New Testament. How does the narrative of salvation and relationship with God unfold throughout the biblical accounts? How do you see yourself fitting into this larger story of God's redemptive plan?

6. Consider the role of the Holy Spirit in bringing you into a relationship with God and empowering your faith walk. How has the Holy Spirit worked in your life to guide, transform, and empower you? Reflect on specific instances where you have experienced the ministry of the Holy Spirit.

7. Reflect on the significance of an eternal relationship with God. How does the prospect of spending eternity with Him impact your present choices, priorities, and values? How can you cultivate a deeper sense of awe and anticipation for the eternal fellowship with God?

8. Consider any challenges or questions that arise from the concept of predestination. How do you reconcile the idea of God's sovereignty and predestined plan with human free will and personal responsibility? How does this tension shape your understanding of your role in cooperating with God's plan?

9. Reflect on the gratitude and awe you feel for being included in God's predestined plan and being called into a relationship with Him. How can you express your thankfulness and live in light of this incredible privilege?

10. How does the understanding of being predestined and chosen by God impact your perspective on evangelism and sharing the message of salvation with others? How does it motivate you to share the hope and love of Christ with those around you?

I AM INCLUDED IN CHRIST!

1. Reflect on the concept of being included in Christ. What does it mean to you personally to be in Christ and to have a deep, intimate connection with Him? How does this understanding shape your identity and self-perception?

2. Consider the significance of being clothed in Christ's righteousness. How does it feel to know that you are covered by His perfect righteousness and that God sees you through the lens of Christ's obedience? Reflect on the assurance and security that come from this truth.

3. Reflect on the blessings and gifts of heaven that are granted to you because you are included in Christ. How does this reality impact your perspective on the abundance and richness of God's provisions in your life? Take a moment to express gratitude for the spiritual blessings you have received through your union with Christ.

4. Consider the role of the Holy Spirit in guarding your spirit and maintaining the connection between you and Christ on a daily, moment-by-moment basis. Reflect on times when you have felt the Spirit's presence and guidance in your life. How does this awareness of the Spirit's work deepen your understanding of being included in Christ?

5. Reflect on the repetition of the phrase "in Christ" throughout the letter to the Ephesians. What do you think Paul is emphasizing by repeatedly using this phrase? How does it reinforce the central theme of being included in Christ and highlight its importance in the believer's life?

6. Consider the confidence that comes from knowing that you are in Christ and that God counts His righteousness toward you. How does this confidence impact your relationship with God and your approach to challenges and difficulties? Reflect on how this assurance can empower you to live boldly and faithfully.

7. Reflect on the unity and oneness that you experience with other believers who are also included in Christ. How does this shared identity in Christ impact your relationships within the body of believers? How does it foster a sense of belonging, unity, and mutual support?

8. Consider how being included in Christ affects your understanding of grace and salvation. Reflect on the transformation that occurs when you receive the message of truth, the gospel of your salvation. How does being in Christ shape your perspective on the purpose and meaning of your life?

9. Reflect on how being included in Christ influences your thoughts, attitudes, and actions. In what ways does your union with Christ manifest in your daily life? How can you intentionally live out this reality more fully and allow it to shape your decisions, relationships, and interactions with others?

10. How does the truth of being included in Christ motivate you to share the message of salvation with others? How does it inspire you to extend God's love, grace, and inclusion to those who may not yet know Him? Consider ways in which you can reflect the inclusive love of Christ to those around you.

I AM MARKED WITH A SEAL!

1. Reflect on the concept of being marked with a seal by God. What does it mean to you to have God's seal of approval and authentication? How does this seal of the Holy Spirit affirm your identity as God's chosen and redeemed child?

2. Consider the role of the Holy Spirit in your life as the seal that God has placed upon you. How does the presence of the Holy Spirit in your heart give you assurance and confidence in your relationship with God? Reflect on the ways in which the Holy Spirit empowers and guides you in your daily walk with Him.

3. Reflect on the significance of God's love in sealing you with His Spirit. How does knowing that God loves you so deeply and intimately impact your understanding of your worth and value in His eyes? How does it shape your perspective on your relationship with Him?

4. Consider the ongoing communion and relationship you have with God through the Holy Spirit. Reflect on the ways in which the Holy Spirit enables you to connect with God, seek His guidance, and experience His presence. How does the Holy Spirit serve as a constant reminder of your connection to God and His faithfulness to you?

5. Reflect on the strength and power that the Holy Spirit provides for you to live a life pleasing to God. How have you experienced the Holy Spirit's transformative work in your thoughts, attitudes, and actions? Reflect on areas of your life where you rely on the Holy Spirit's guidance and empowerment.

6. Consider the promise of the Holy Spirit as a guarantee of your inheritance in Christ. How does the presence of the Holy Spirit within you assure you of the future redemption and eternal life that God has prepared for His children? Reflect on the hope and security that come from this promise.

7. Reflect on how the seal of the Holy Spirit sets you apart as belonging to God. How does this seal impact your interactions with the world and your identity as a representative of Christ? How does it influence the choices you make and the way you live your life?

8. Consider the praise and glory that is due to God because of His sealing work in your life. How does the seal of the Holy Spirit point others to the greatness and faithfulness of God? Reflect on ways in which you can live a life that brings praise and glory to God in response to His sealing work in you.

9. Reflect on the privilege and responsibility of having the Holy Spirit dwell within you. How does this reality shape your attitude toward your relationship with God and your commitment to live in obedience to Him? How can you nurture and cultivate a deeper connection with the Holy Spirit in your daily life?

10. Reflect on the grace and mercy of God in sealing you with His Spirit. How does this seal remind you of the unmerited favor and forgiveness you have received through Christ? How does it inspire you to extend grace and love to others, knowing that you too have been marked and sealed by God's love?

I AM CALLED TO HOPE!

1. Reflect on your understanding of hope. How has this reflection challenged or expanded your perspective on what true hope means in the context of your faith in Christ? How does this understanding of hope differ from wishful thinking or uncertainty?

2. Consider the confidence that comes from knowing and trusting in the promises of God. How does this assurance impact your daily life and perspective? Reflect on specific promises of God that bring you hope and how they shape your outlook on the future.

3. Reflect on the statement that hope in Christ is not based on uncertainty but on the certainty of God's faithfulness. How does this perspective shift your mindset and approach to challenges and difficulties in life? How does it provide strength and perseverance in times of uncertainty?

4. Consider the call to trust in God's Word and obey His commands as part of living in the hope to which you are called. Reflect on the relationship between hope and obedience. How does your confidence in God's promises influence your willingness to follow His guidance and live according to His will?

5. Reflect on the depth of knowing God fully as part of the hope He has called you into. How does your growing knowledge of God and intimacy with Him deepen your sense of hope and trust in His plans for your life? How does it shape your relationship with Him on a personal level?

6. Consider the contrast between wishful thinking and confident hope. How does this distinction impact your expectations and mindset as you approach prayer, seeking God's guidance, and believing in His provision? Reflect on areas in your life where you can align your thinking more closely with confident hope in God.

7. Reflect on the eternal hope you have in Christ and the assurance of a place prepared for you. How does this hope shape your perspective on the temporary challenges and trials of life? How does it bring comfort, peace, and a sense of purpose in the midst of difficult circumstances?

8. Consider how your understanding and experience of hope in Christ can inspire and encourage others. Reflect on ways in which you can share this confident hope with those around you who may be struggling or in need of encouragement. How can your life and words be a testimony of the hope you have in Christ?

9. Reflect on the faithfulness and sovereignty of God as the foundation of your hope. How does acknowledging God's power and authority over all things strengthen your hope? How can you remind yourself of His faithfulness and trustworthiness during times of doubt or uncertainty?

10. Consider the prayer for the eyes of your heart to be enlightened to know the hope to which you are called. How can you actively seek a deeper understanding and experience of this hope? What spiritual practices, study, or reflection can help you grow in your confidence and trust in God's promises?

I AM POWERFUL!

1. Reflect on your understanding of the power available to you through the Holy Spirit. How does this reflection challenge your perception of your own power and abilities? How does knowing that you have access to the same power that raised Christ from the dead impact your perspective on your potential and capabilities?

2. Consider the connection between knowing the hope to which you are called and understanding the power available to you. How does knowing and embracing the hope of your calling empower you to live a life that reflects God's power? Reflect on specific areas of your life where you need to rely on God's power more fully.

3. Reflect on any areas of defeat or feelings of inadequacy in your life. How does the knowledge of God's incomparably great power for believers challenge and change your perspective in those areas? How can you actively tap into that power to overcome obstacles, insecurities, and challenges in your life?

4. Consider the significance of the power that raised Christ from the dead and its implications for your daily life. Reflect on the authority and dominion that God has bestowed upon Jesus and how that same power is available to you. How does this understanding impact your approach to spiritual warfare, personal growth, and living a life that honors God?

5. Reflect on the contrast between relying on your own strength and relying on the power of God. How does recognizing your own limitations and weaknesses shift your dependence to God's power? How can you surrender more fully to His power and allow it to work through you in all aspects of your life?

6. Consider the importance of living in God's power for the advancement of His kingdom. Reflect on the opportunities and impact that could arise if you fully embraced and utilized the power He has granted you. How can you align your actions, decisions, and priorities with the reality of God's power in your life?

7. Reflect on the relationship between living in God's power and experiencing hope and joy. How does embracing His power transform your perspective, outlook, and emotional well-being? How can you cultivate a mindset that consistently relies on His power, leading to a more hopeful and joy-filled life?

8. Consider the potential barriers or hindrances that prevent you from fully embracing and living in God's power. Reflect on any doubts, fears, or self-limiting beliefs that may be holding you back. How can you surrender those obstacles to God and allow His power to overcome them?

9. Reflect on the invitation to live in God's power on a daily, moment-by-moment basis. How can you develop a deeper awareness of His presence and power in your everyday life? How can you intentionally seek His guidance and empowerment in your decisions, relationships, and responsibilities?

10. Consider the invitation to live a life that reflects the power of God. How can you be a witness and testimony to His power in your words, actions, and character? How can you point others to the source of your power and inspire them to seek a relationship with God?

I AM VALUED!

1. Reflect on the depth of God's love and value for you as expressed through sending His Son to die for your sins. How does this understanding impact your perception of your worth and value in His eyes? How does it challenge any feelings of unworthiness or self-doubt?

2. Consider the significance of being adopted into God's family and the inheritance that comes with it. Reflect on the spiritual treasures and blessings that God has bestowed upon you as His child. How does recognizing and embracing this inheritance change your perspective on earthly possessions and achievements?

3. Reflect on the role of grace in God's valuation of you. How does understanding that your value is not based on your own efforts or accomplishments, but solely on His grace, impact your self-worth and identity? How can you extend that same grace to yourself and others?

4. Consider the assurance and security that comes from knowing that your value and inheritance are guaranteed by the deposit of the Holy Spirit. Reflect on the unchanging nature of God's love and the eternal nature of your inheritance. How does this knowledge bring peace and confidence to your daily life?

5. Reflect on the ways in which your understanding of being valued by God affects your interactions with others. How can you extend love, grace, and value to those around you, recognizing their worth as fellow recipients of God's love and inheritance?

6. Consider any challenges or obstacles that may hinder you from fully embracing your value in God's eyes. Reflect on any negative self-perceptions or external pressures that may distort your understanding of your worth. How can you surrender those challenges to God and allow His truth to shape your self-perception?

7. Reflect on the contrast between earthly treasures and the spiritual treasures of God's inheritance. How can you cultivate a mindset that prioritizes spiritual blessings and values over material possessions and achievements? How can you invest in the eternal rather than the temporary?

8. Consider the impact of knowing and embracing your value in God's eyes on your overall well-being and self-care. How does recognizing your worth as a child of God influence your self-esteem, self-care practices, and mental and emotional health? How can you prioritize your spiritual well-being and nurture a positive self-image rooted in God's love?

9. Reflect on the invitation to walk through life with the knowledge of your value in God's eyes. How can you remind yourself daily of His love and the significance He places on you? How can you allow this knowledge to shape your attitudes, actions, and choices?

10. Consider how you can reflect God's love and value in your interactions with others. How can you encourage and uplift those around you, affirming their worth and value as fellow children of God? How can you be an instrument of God's love and grace in the lives of others?

I AM ALIVE!

1. Reflect on the depth of God's mercy and love that led Him to make you alive with Christ. How does this realization impact your understanding of your own identity and purpose? How does it shape your view of God's character and His desire for a relationship with you?

2. Consider the significance of being born into a sinful nature and the need for repentance and turning to God. Reflect on your own journey of recognizing the errors of your ways and embracing God's forgiveness and redemption. How has this transformation affected your perspective on sin, righteousness, and the pursuit of a life aligned with God's will?

3. Reflect on the concept of being made alive with Christ and the transformative power of His resurrection. How does the indwelling presence of the Holy Spirit in your life manifest as newness of life and spiritual vitality? How has this new life impacted your thoughts, desires, and actions?

4. Consider the contrast between the cravings of the flesh and the fulfillment found in God's spirit. Reflect on the emptiness and temporary satisfaction that comes from gratifying worldly desires versus the lasting fulfillment and purpose that comes from being alive in Christ. How can you cultivate a mindset that prioritizes spiritual growth and seeks satisfaction in God's presence?

5. Reflect on the concept of being adopted as a child of God and the significance of being sealed with His spirit. How does this understanding of your identity as a beloved child of God impact your sense of belonging, security, and value? How can you nurture a deeper connection with God as your Heavenly Father and embrace your identity as His beloved child?

6. Consider the role of grace in your salvation and new life in Christ. Reflect on the undeserved nature of God's grace and how it shapes your understanding of salvation and relationship with Him. How can you extend that same grace to others and embody a life marked by forgiveness and compassion?

7. Reflect on the mystery and wonder of being made alive with Christ, surpassing human understanding. How does this truth deepen your awe

and reverence for God? How can you cultivate a sense of wonder and gratitude for the spiritual transformation and new life that you have experienced?

8. Consider the impact of being alive with Christ on your daily walk and relationship with Him. How does this truth shape your perspective on trials, challenges, and the pursuit of holiness? How can you live in the fullness of this new life, relying on God's strength and guidance each day?

9. Reflect on the responsibility and privilege of being made alive with Christ. How can you actively participate in God's kingdom and His work in the world? How can you share the message of new life in Christ with others and invite them into a relationship with Him?

10. Consider the joy and gratitude that comes from being made alive with Christ. How can you cultivate a spirit of thankfulness and celebration for the transformation and blessings you have received? How can you share your testimony of new life with others, pointing them towards the hope and restoration found in Jesus?

I AM RAISED UP!

1. Reflect on the concept of being raised up with Christ and seated in the heavenly realms. How does this truth impact your perspective on your identity and purpose? How does it challenge or transform your understanding of your worth and significance?

2. Consider the contrast between your physical condition and your spiritual position in Christ. How does the assurance of your fixed spiritual condition at the right hand of the Father provide strength and stability in the midst of challenging circumstances? How can you shift your focus from the problems of the physical to the truth of your spiritual identity in Christ?

3. Reflect on the idea of finding your identity in Christ rather than in external factors or worldly achievements. How does this perspective shape your view of success, worth, and validation? How can you cultivate a mindset that relies on your identity and status in Christ rather than seeking approval or recognition from others?

4. Consider the power and strength that come from being raised up and seated with Christ. How does this truth empower you to overcome challenges, temptations, and spiritual battles? How can you actively tap into the resources and authority you have in Christ to live a victorious Christian life?

5. Reflect on the role of faith in embracing your status and privilege in Christ. How does faith enable you to trust that everything you need is found in Christ? How can you nurture and deepen your faith in order to fully embrace your identity and position in Him?

6. Consider the significance of being accepted as an adopted child of God and seated with His Son. How does this truth shape your understanding of God's love and acceptance? How can you cultivate a deeper appreciation for the privilege and honor of being part of God's family?

7. Reflect on the implications of being raised up with Christ for your daily walk and relationship with Him. How does this truth impact your perspective on obedience, holiness, and spiritual growth? How can you live in a manner that reflects your heavenly position and brings glory to God?

8. Consider the joy and gratitude that come from being raised up and seated with Christ. How can you cultivate a spirit of thankfulness and celebration for the blessings and privileges you have received? How can you share this truth with others and invite them to experience the transformative power of being raised up in Christ?

9. Reflect on the eternal perspective that being raised up with Christ offers. How does this truth shape your view of life's trials, hardships, and the transient nature of earthly things? How can you live with a focus on the eternal and invest your time, energy, and resources in things that have lasting value?

10. Consider the responsibility and calling that come with being raised up and seated with Christ. How can you actively participate in God's purposes and His kingdom work? How can you use your position and influence to bring about positive change, share the Gospel, and impact the lives of others?

I AM GOD'S HANDIWORK!

1. Reflect on the truth that you are God's handiwork, created for a purpose. How does this truth impact your understanding of your identity, worth, and significance? How can you embrace and celebrate your uniqueness, knowing that God has intentionally crafted you for His good works?

2. Consider the ways in which fear, past failures, or the opinions of others have hindered you from fulfilling the good works God has prepared for you. How can you overcome these obstacles and step out in faith, trusting in God's provision, guidance, and qualification for the tasks He has set before you?

3. Reflect on the power of God's voice and the importance of seeking His approval above all others. How can you cultivate a deeper sensitivity to God's voice and discern His leading in your life? How can you silence the voices of doubt, rejection, and negativity that may distract you from fulfilling your purpose in Him?

4. Consider the significance of hearing God's commendation, "Well done, good and faithful servant." How does this motivate you to persevere in fulfilling the good works God has prepared for you? How can you stay focused on His affirmation rather than seeking validation or recognition from others?

5. Reflect on the role of maintaining a close relationship with God in fulfilling your purpose. How can you prioritize and nurture your relationship with Him through prayer, Bible study, worship, and fellowship? How does staying connected to the Creator of the universe equip and empower you to accomplish His works?

6. Consider the impact of your good works on the world around you and the glory they bring to God. How can you actively seek opportunities to do good, showing God's love and character to others? How can you be a vessel through which His power and grace flow to those in need?

7. Reflect on the importance of perseverance and faithfulness in fulfilling your purpose. How can you cultivate a resilient and steadfast spirit, even in the face of challenges, setbacks, or discouragement? How can you rely on God's strength and promises to keep running the race and finishing well?

8. Consider the alignment between your gifts, talents, experiences, and the good works God has prepared for you. How can you discern and utilize your unique abilities and opportunities to make a positive impact in the world? How can you continually seek God's guidance in aligning your strengths with His purposes?

9. Reflect on the joy and fulfillment that come from embracing and living out your purpose as God's handiwork. How can you cultivate a mindset of gratitude and contentment, finding joy in the journey of fulfilling His good works? How can you encourage and inspire others to discover and embrace their own God-given purposes?

10. Consider the eternal significance of the good works you do in Christ. How can you keep an eternal perspective, recognizing that your actions and obedience have far-reaching consequences beyond this present life? How can you invest your time, resources, and energy in things that have lasting value and contribute to God's eternal kingdom?

I AM BROUGHT NEAR!

1. Reflect on your past state of being far away from God. How did sin and barriers hinder your relationship with Him? What was the turning point that led you to accept Jesus as your Savior and be brought near to God? How has this transformation impacted your life and perspective?

2. Consider the significance of the blood of Christ in bringing you near to God. How does the sacrifice of Jesus on the cross remove the barriers and sins that separated you from God? How does His blood continually cleanse and restore your relationship with Him?

3. Reflect on the ongoing work of grace in your life. How does God's grace continue to remove the barriers that your sinful nature tries to put up? How can you actively cooperate with God's grace and surrender to His will, allowing Him to draw you even closer to Himself?

4. Consider the role of submission and resistance in your relationship with God. How can you submit yourself to God and resist the temptations and attacks of the devil? How does drawing near to God result in His nearness to you? How can you cultivate a lifestyle of drawing near to God through prayer, worship, and obedience?

5. Reflect on the blessings and abundance that come from being brought near to God. How has your relationship with Him filled you with good things and brought fulfillment to your life? How can you appreciate and celebrate the benefits of living in His presence and experiencing His goodness?

6. Consider the invitation and privilege of dwelling in God's courts and experiencing His presence. How does this reality deepen your gratitude and awe towards God? How can you intentionally create space and time to dwell in His presence, seeking communion with Him and enjoying the intimacy of your relationship?

7. Reflect on the broader implications of being brought near to God. How does this closeness with Him impact your identity, purpose, and perspective on life? How can you share the joy of being brought near to God with others, inviting them into a relationship with Him as well?

8. Consider the ongoing journey of drawing near to God. How can you continually pursue a deeper relationship with Him, seeking to know Him more intimately and experience His presence in new ways? How can you cultivate a heart of gratitude and humility, recognizing the privilege of being brought near and cherishing the ongoing growth in your relationship with God?

9. Reflect on the transformative power of being brought near to God. How has your relationship with Him changed your thoughts, attitudes, and actions? How can you allow His nearness to shape your character and influence the way you interact with others and navigate life's challenges?

10. Consider the eternal significance of being brought near to God. How does this closeness with Him impact your perspective on eternity and the hope you have in Christ? How can you live with a sense of purpose and anticipation, knowing that your relationship with God will continue to deepen and flourish throughout all eternity?

I AM A FELLOW CITIZEN!

1. Reflect on your understanding of being a foreigner and stranger before coming to faith in Christ. How did your relationship with God and your sense of belonging change when you became a fellow citizen with God's people? How does this new identity as a member of God's family impact your perspective on your spiritual heritage and the promises of God?

2. Consider the unifying power of Christ's sacrifice and resurrection. How does Jesus' redemptive work on the cross bridge the gap between Hebrews and Gentiles, bringing all of humanity together as one body? How does this unity in Christ challenge your preconceptions and prejudices, promoting a sense of equality and shared identity among believers?

3. Reflect on the role of the Holy Spirit in granting access to the Father. How does the indwelling presence of the Holy Spirit break down barriers and create a sense of unity among God's people? How does the Spirit's work in your life and the lives of others reinforce the reality of being fellow citizens and members of the same spiritual family?

4. Consider the significance of the gospel's global reach and its impact on your identity as a fellow citizen. How does the command to make disciples of all nations emphasize the inclusivity of God's kingdom and the diversity within His people? How does your participation in spreading the gospel and making disciples contribute to the sense of fellowship and shared citizenship among believers?

5. Reflect on the privilege and responsibility of sharing in the heritage of God's people. How does your faith in Christ connect you to the rich history and promises of God's dealings with His people throughout the Old Testament? How does this shared heritage strengthen and challenge your faith, reminding you of God's faithfulness and the need to walk in obedience and unity with fellow believers?

6. Consider the implications of being a fellow citizen with God's people for your daily life and relationships. How does this identity influence the way you interact with other believers and approach challenges within the body of Christ? How can you foster a sense of unity, love, and support among fellow citizens, regardless of cultural backgrounds or differences?

7. Reflect on the diversity within the body of Christ and its significance in your understanding of being a fellow citizen. How does the inclusion of people from various nations, cultures, and backgrounds enrich your experience as a member of God's family? How can you appreciate and celebrate this diversity while fostering unity and understanding among fellow citizens?

8. Consider the ongoing journey of living out your identity as a fellow citizen. How can you actively participate in the community of believers, nurturing relationships, and contributing to the growth and edification of the body of Christ? How does embracing your role as a fellow citizen impact your sense of belonging, purpose, and commitment to God's kingdom work?

9. Reflect on the eternal implications of being a fellow citizen with God's people. How does this identity shape your perspective on eternity and the hope of being united with believers from all nations in the presence of God? How can this anticipation of the future kingdom influence your priorities and actions in the present?

10. Consider the role of gratitude and stewardship in light of being a fellow citizen. How can you express gratitude for the privilege of belonging to God's family and participating in His kingdom? How can you steward this identity well by living a life that honors God, reflects His love, and extends His invitation of citizenship to others?

I AM A MEMBER OF GOD'S HOUSEHOLD!

1. Reflect on your understanding of being a member of God's household. How does this concept of belonging to God's family impact your sense of identity, purpose, and responsibility within the body of Christ? How does it shape your relationships with fellow believers?

2. Consider the dynamics of family life and how they apply to your experience as a member of God's household. How does the reality of imperfection and occasional hurt within families challenge your expectations and interactions with other believers? How can you foster a culture of grace, forgiveness, and unconditional love within the community of believers?

3. Reflect on the inclusivity of God's household. How does the unity of believers across different churches, cities, and nations emphasize the universal nature of the body of Christ? How does this perspective challenge any tendencies towards exclusivity or division in your own thinking and actions?

4. Consider the role of the Holy Spirit in unifying and building up the household of God. How does the presence and work of the Holy Spirit empower believers to live in harmony, love, and mutual support? How can you actively yield to the guidance of the Holy Spirit in your relationships with other members of God's household?

5. Reflect on the rich heritage and foundation of the apostles, prophets, and Christ Himself. How does their example and teachings shape your understanding of faith, discipleship, and the mission of the church? How can you draw from this heritage to deepen your own commitment and contribution to the household of God?

6. Consider the global and historical dimensions of God's household. How does your membership in God's family connect you to believers across time and geographical boundaries? How can you learn from the experiences, testimonies, and wisdom of believers who have gone before you, as well as those from different cultural backgrounds or traditions?

7. Reflect on the future hope and unity of God's household. How does the anticipation of the ultimate reunion in Christ's return impact your perspective on the challenges, conflicts, and divisions that may arise within the body of Christ? How can you cultivate a sense of unity, hope, and eternal perspective within the family of God?

8. Consider the significance of love and acceptance within God's household. How can you actively demonstrate love, kindness, and hospitality towards your fellow believers? How can you create an environment where individuals feel valued, supported, and encouraged to grow in their faith and relationship with God?

9. Reflect on the unique calling and purpose of God's household. How does being a member of God's family shape your understanding of your role in fulfilling the mission of the church? How can you use your gifts, talents, and resources to contribute to the growth, edification, and outreach of the household of God?

10. Consider the gratitude and responsibility that come with being a member of God's household. How can you express thankfulness for the privilege of being part of God's family and actively steward this membership for His glory? How can you actively engage with and invest in the lives of fellow believers, seeking to build strong, authentic, and life-giving relationships within the household of God?

I AM A DWELLING!

1. Reflect on the significance of having the Holy Spirit dwelling within you. How does the indwelling of the Holy Spirit shape your understanding of your identity, purpose, and potential as a believer? How does it impact your daily life and decision-making?

2. Consider the transformative power of the Holy Spirit in your life. How has the Holy Spirit worked in your heart, transforming it from a heart of stone to a heart of flesh? Reflect on specific instances where the Holy Spirit has guided you, convicted you, or empowered you to follow God's will.

3. Reflect on the role of the Holy Spirit as a guide and source of truth. How do you actively seek the guidance and leading of the Holy Spirit in your life? How can you cultivate a deeper sensitivity to the promptings and teachings of the Holy Spirit? In what ways can you align your thoughts and desires with what the Spirit desires?

4. Consider the intimate relationship between the Holy Spirit, Jesus, and the Father. How does this unity within the Godhead impact your understanding of the indwelling of the Holy Spirit? How does it shape your relationship with Jesus and your perception of God's love and involvement in your life?

5. Reflect on the concept of living in accordance with the Spirit. What does it mean for your mind to be set on what the Spirit desires? How can you actively cooperate with the Holy Spirit in cultivating a life that aligns with God's will, values, and purposes?

6. Consider the peace and life that the Holy Spirit brings to your life. Reflect on the ways in which the Holy Spirit has brought you comfort, guidance, and assurance in challenging times. How can you lean on the Holy Spirit's presence to find strength and peace in the midst of life's difficulties?

7. Reflect on the future hope and transformation promised by the Holy Spirit. How does the assurance of the Holy Spirit's presence and power give you confidence in the resurrection of your mortal body? How does it shape your perspective on eternity and your purpose in the present?

8. Consider the responsibility that comes with having the Holy Spirit dwelling within you. How can you honor the presence of the Holy Spirit by living a life that reflects God's character and values? How can you yield to the Holy Spirit's work of sanctification, allowing Him to shape you into the person God has called you to be?

9. Reflect on the gift of new life that comes through the Holy Spirit. How has the Holy Spirit brought about transformation and renewal in your life? How can you share the good news of the Spirit's life-giving work with others and invite them into a relationship with Christ?

10. Consider the ongoing relationship and dependence on the Holy Spirit in your journey of faith. How can you cultivate a deeper intimacy with the Holy Spirit through prayer, studying God's Word, and engaging in spiritual disciplines? How can you daily surrender to the leading and empowering of the Holy Spirit, allowing Him to work in and through you for God's glory?

LAST WORD

1. Reflect on the significance of being led by the Spirit of God. In what ways have you experienced the guidance and leading of the Holy Spirit in your life? How does being led by the Spirit shape your decisions, priorities, and actions?

2. Consider the freedom and assurance that comes from being adopted as a child of God. How does the presence of the Holy Spirit in your life dispel fear and bring about a sense of security and belonging? How can you cultivate a deeper understanding and experience of your identity as a beloved child of God?

3. Reflect on the testimony of the Holy Spirit within you. How does the Spirit bear witness with your spirit that you are indeed a child of God? In what ways do you experience the presence and confirmation of the Holy Spirit in your relationship with God and your understanding of your identity?

4. Consider the inheritance and co-heirship with Christ that you have as a child of God. Reflect on the privileges, blessings, and promises that are available to you through your adoption into God's family. How does knowing that you are an heir of God impact your perspective on life, purpose, and eternity?

5. Reflect on the transformative work of the Holy Spirit in manifesting the gifts of God in your life. How have you seen the Holy Spirit's power and gifting at work in and through you? How can you actively cooperate with the Holy Spirit's work of empowering, equipping, and transforming you to live in alignment with God's purposes?

6. Consider the confidence and victory that come from knowing your identity as a child of God and the indwelling presence of the Holy Spirit. How does this knowledge and assurance empower you to face challenges, overcome obstacles, and live a life of faith and obedience? How can you continually remind yourself of your true identity and rely on the Holy Spirit's strength and guidance in every aspect of your life?

7. Reflect on the implications of being a child of God and having the Holy Spirit's presence in your life. How does this reality impact your relationships, interactions, and responsibilities within the body of Christ and in the world? How can you share the love, grace, and truth of God with others, inviting them into a relationship with Him and the transformative power of the Holy Spirit?

LEADING A SMALL GROUP BIBLE STUDY

Leading a small group Bible study is a fulfilling and impactful way to nurture spiritual growth and build a vibrant community of believers. Small group settings offer a space for deeper exploration of God's Word, meaningful discussions, and mutual support among members. If you're considering leading a small group or looking to enhance your current leadership skills, this reflection provides practical tips and strategies to help you effectively lead a small group Bible study.

Pray and Seek God's Guidance:

The foundation of any successful small group Bible study is seeking God's guidance through prayer. Before every meeting, take time to pray for the group members, their individual needs, and the study itself. Involve other group members in praying, allowing a collective seeking of God's wisdom and understanding.

Select an Engaging Study:

Choose a Bible study that aligns with the group's needs and spiritual growth goals. Consider the group's interests, spiritual maturity levels, and any specific topics or themes they want to explore. Engaging studies can include books of the Bible, thematic studies, character studies, or topical issues relevant to the group's lives.

Set Clear Objectives:

Establish clear objectives for the small group Bible study. Define the purpose of the study, the desired outcomes, and the schedule for completing the material. Clearly communicate these objectives to the group members to keep everyone on the same page.

Create a Welcoming Environment:

Foster a warm and inclusive atmosphere in your small group. Make sure everyone feels welcomed, valued, and safe to share their thoughts and questions. Encourage open dialogue and respect for differing perspectives, ensuring that everyone has an opportunity to participate.

Be Prepared:

Thoroughly prepare for each session by studying the material in advance. Familiarize yourself with the study content, key Scriptures, and discussion questions. Anticipate potential questions that may arise during the study and be ready to address them with clarity and biblical insight.

Facilitate Engaging Discussions:

As the leader, your role is to facilitate meaningful discussions that encourage group members to delve deeper into the Word of God. Ask open-ended questions that provoke thought and encourage personal reflection. Allow members to share their insights and experiences, ensuring that the conversation remains centered on the study's focus.

Encourage Participation:

Encourage active participation from all group members. Avoid dominating the discussion, and instead, give space for everyone to share their thoughts. Be patient and allow for moments of silence, as some may need time to process and respond.

Foster Accountability and Prayer:

Promote a culture of accountability and prayer within the group. Encourage members to share their prayer requests and follow up on these requests in subsequent meetings. Ensure that the group remains committed to praying for one another and supporting each other through life's challenges.

Embrace Flexibility:

Be flexible in your approach to leading the small group Bible study. Allow the Holy Spirit to guide the discussions and take the study in unexpected directions. Remain open to adjustments in the study plan if the group's needs change or if the Spirit leads you to explore a different aspect of the study material.

Lead by Example:

As the leader, model a genuine and humble pursuit of God's Word in your own life. Demonstrate a desire to grow spiritually and to apply the truths of the Bible in your daily walk with Christ. Your authenticity will inspire and motivate the group members to do the same.

Conclusion:

Leading a small group Bible study is a privilege and an opportunity to make a lasting impact on the lives of fellow believers. By praying fervently, selecting engaging studies, and fostering a welcoming environment, you can create a space for spiritual growth, community building, and deeper understanding of God's Word. As you lead with humility, flexibility, and a heart for authentic fellowship, your small group Bible study will flourish and become a source of joy and transformation for everyone involved.

ABOUT THE AUTHOR

Sean Slagle was born and raised in Kentucky. In 1990 he moved to Indiana and completed his B.A. in English from Indiana University East. He continued to write while working various and, at time, multiple jobs. After earning an M.A. in Secondary Education from Ball State University, he has taught high school English, as well as served as a basketball coach, softball coach, track coach, and drama director. He was also an adjunct professor at Indiana Wesleyan University for ten years.

You can learn more about him and his works at www.seanslagle.com

Michael James is the pastor of a small church in Short Ridge, Kentucky, a community in the foothills of Appalachia. Life seems normal until Judd Simmons, a local drug lord, tries to kill his own family and Michael is called on to help, which has consequences beyond that one evening. Alycen Loveless is a new journalist at The Outlook. She rushes onto the scene to report on the terrors the family faced. Later, as she delves into the town's dark side and fears, she finds an unlikely romance with the pastor from that fateful night. But love has a hard time blossoming when the couple is stalked, threatened, and harassed to the point that Michael questions if he can take another man's life.

Learn more at www.agfpublishingcompany.com

MORE FROM AGF PUBLISHING AND NORTHSIDE BOOKS & MEDIA

Seize the Moment represents an intentional mindset for followers of Jesus Christ to strengthen their spiritual vitality and live on mission. Living in this mindset involves viewing every circumstance as a providential opportunity to grow closer to Jesus, as His yokefellow, and being aware of the Holy Spirit's promptings for faithful living. The method is simple—make time every day for the reading of a chapter of God's Word, followed by a focused meditation on an aspect of that chapter, concluding with an invitation to prayerfully apply God's Word in your day, for His glory.

Find this and more at www.agfpublishingcompany.com

BOOKS 1 AND 2 OF THE LIVE TODAY DISCIPLESHIP TRILOGY

Dr. Jerry Ingalls built this work on the athletic imagery of the New Testament, anchored it in the expository study of 2 Peter 1's teaching of "His precious and magnificent promises," and applied it through his intensive pastoral study of how to personally and corporately train for godliness through 40 promises of God found in the Bible. You, as well as the other members of God's team in your local church or community, can learn to apply every Word of God to your daily life through an intensive 40-day training regimen, called "The 40 Promises in 40 Days Challenge!"

Live on Mission Today teaches you how to live a Christ-centered life by training you to live according to the training regimen of a Christian soldier. This book was designed intentionally to prepare you to be ready, at any time, to accomplish God's calling upon your life, anywhere you are commanded to go. You are invited to learn how to train yourself, according to God's wisdom, to grow strong in God's grace so that you can live on mission today, without being distracted by that which is not God's priority for your life. This book teaches you, from a soldier's perspective, how to live your life effectively and fruitfully for God's mission in your daily life – Live on Mission Today!

AGF PUBLISHING LLC

AGF PUBLISHING LLC seeks to entertain, educate, inform, and inspire people of all ages. Our various imprints reach readers where they are in life's journey.

Learn more about the company and all its offerings at www.agfpublishingcompany.com

NORTHSIDE
AN AGF IMPRINT

NORTHSIDE BOOKS & MEDIA

AN AGF PUBLISHING IMPRINT

At Northside Books & Media, we strive to be a beacon of light and inspiration, serving as a source of encouragement and empowerment for Christians around the world. We believe in the transformative power of literature and its ability to shape hearts, minds, and communities. Our mission is to provide literature that not only entertains but also edifies, equips, and encourages believers to live out their faith with passion and purpose.

Join us on this remarkable journey as we explore the vast realm of Christian fiction and nonfiction. Discover new authors, embark on thrilling adventures, gain fresh perspectives, and deepen your understanding of the Christian faith. Northside Books & Media is your trusted companion in your pursuit of spiritual growth and inspiration.

Look for more titles, author information and call for manuscripts at www.agfpublishingcompany.com

www.ingramcontent.com/pod-product-compliance
Lightning Source LLC
LaVergne TN
LVHW010700110826
845149LV00014B/3186

* 9 7 8 1 9 5 5 7 0 9 1 3 2 *